CLASSIC WRITINGS FROM BUILDERS OF OUR FAITH

Architects
of the
Enduring

~

Classic Writings
from Builders of
Our Faith

~

Edited and Compiled
by
Neil B. Wiseman

Neil B. Wiseman
Falcon
2004

Beacon Hill Press of Kansas City
Kansas City, Missouri

Cover Design: Paul Franitza

Note: The writings included herein have been slightly modified to conform to current stylistic practices. Further, Scripture references have been inserted where needed, and certain song lyrics, where indicated, have been taken from *Sing to the Lord* (STTL), Kansas City: Lillenas Publishing Co., 1993.

Chapter titles are based on "Take Time to Be Holy" (STTL, 512).

All Scripture quotations not otherwise designated are from the King James Version.

Permission to quote from the following copyrighted versions of the Bible is acknowledged with appreciation:

The *Amplified New Testament* (AMP.), copyright © 1954, 1958, 1987 by The Lockman Foundation.

The Jerusalem Bible (JB), copyright © 1966 by Darton, Longman & Todd, Ltd., and Doubleday, a division of Bantam Doubleday Dell Publishing Group, Inc.

New American Standard Bible® (NASB®), © copyright The Lockman Foundation 1960, 1962, 1963, 1968, 1971, 1972, 1973, 1975, 1977, 1995.

The New English Bible (NEB). Copyright © by the Delegates of the Oxford University Press and the Syndics of the Cambridge University Press, 1961, 1970. Reprinted by permission.

Holy Bible, New International Version® (NIV®). Copyright © 1973, 1978, 1984 by International Bible Society. Used by permission of Zondervan Publishing House. All rights reserved

New King James Version (NKJV). Copyright © 1979, 1980, 1982 Thomas Nelson, Inc.

Revised Standard Version (RSV) of the Bible, copyright 1946, 1952, 1971 by the Division of Christian Education of the National Council of the Churches of Christ in the USA.

The Message (TM). Copyright © 1993. Used by permission of NavPress Publishing Group.

Library of Congress Cataloging-in-Publication Data

Classic writings from builders of our faith / compiled and edited by Neil B. Wiseman.
   p. cm. — (Architects of the enduring)
   ISBN 0-8341-1896-3
   1. Christian life—Nazarene authors. I. Wiseman, Neil B. II. Series.
BV4501.3 .C53 2001
248.4'8799—dc21

2001025888

10   9   8   7   6   5   4   3   2   1

Contents

The singing of the early Nazarenes drew friends and neighbors to their services. From the beginning they wrote, published, and sang songs communicating the Holiness message. Pictured are two early Nazarene hymnals, *Waves of Glory* (first published in 1907) and *Pentecostal Praises* (first published in 1911).

Preface

Unlike most religious movements, the Church of the Nazarene started in the hearts of people long before any denominational organization was ever considered. God started it all by lighting Holiness fires in human hearts in Brooklyn, Chicago, Los Angles, Nashville, and a thousand places in between.

This Church of the Nazarene actually started at makeshift altars in homes, tents, prayer meetings, spiritually dead churches, and sometimes in fields as farmers did their work. The beginning came as people all over the United States were experiencing a hunger for more of God than they had known. Their common bond was their seeking the Holy Spirit's sanctifying grace by faith as a second definite work of grace that cleansed their hearts from sin and empowered them to live holy lives of complete devotement to God. As they came into this holy fullness and shared their discovery, they were increasingly unwelcome in the established churches of their time.

So they started associations, camp meetings, and finally congregations. That means that the early days of the Church of the Nazarene across North America were filled with happy finders of holiness. It was understood that if you had been sanctified holy, you were welcome to join the Nazarenes. As a result, merging groups from the east and the west met in Chicago in 1907, and other groups from the south joined at Pilot Point, Texas, in 1908. Though the actual organization of the denomination was put into place at Pilot Point, the movement was much more than an organization or new denomination.

Very early in the development of the movement, certainly before 1907, Holiness people became acquainted and kept connected through the printed page. The printing press and mail service were used to spread the word, to explain the doctrine, to introduce leaders, and to "preserve the work."

In the days before radio, TV, and jet travel, people read more than they do now. And in order to meet those reading needs and to fan the interest, their spiritual leaders became effective writers. Writing as a communication delivery system for the Holiness message took weekly journals into people's homes, produced Sunday School curriculum for developing the new converts and more veteran believers, and caused the Nazarene Publishing House to be valued as a constant source of Holiness literature. The idea was to keep writing about the message so it would be strengthened, understood, and lived by Nazarenes everywhere.

Classic Writings from Builders of Our Faith attempts to introduce contemporary readers to important influential writers and their writings from the Nazarene past. The use of the word *classic* does not intend to communicate the idea that these writings are old and uninteresting. Neither are these writings all that was written on these subjects—rather what we publish here is representative of a whole body of instructive literature.

The book has several purposes. It endeavors to (1) show how timeless the Holiness message is, (2) provide a primer for new Nazarenes to help them cherish their Holiness heritage, (3) provide a unique devotional resource, (4) help all hear the basics again and rejoice in them, (5) and encourage all to celebrate the spiritual legacy the builders of our faith left us.

The companion book, *Uncommon Stories from Everyday Nazarenes*—the stories of ordinary people who did extraordinary things to make the Church of the Nazarene strong and great—should be read side by side with this book. This book is conceptual, and that book demonstrates how the doctrine works in consecrated lives.

Having been taken in 1932 as a newborn to my first Nazarene service and since then having been to hundreds of worship services, revivals, camp meetings, and district and general assemblies, I remember hearing in person many of the contributors to this book. And having been in Nazarene ministry service for 45 years, I have read their books and heard stories about every one of them. I am pleased to introduce these shapers of our faith to your reading and strongly recommend that in the details of your life you live out what they wrote.

Blessings and peace,
Neil B. Wiseman

Street meetings were a frequent occurrence on Sunday afternoons in the early days of the Church of the Nazarene. In this picture Nazarene Publishing House employees used the company truck to transport Christian workers to their outdoor meeting.

Faith to Be a Nazarene

If you can see the oak tree in the acorn
  And fields of wheat in one handful of grain,
If you can see the fountain on the hillside
  Become the river spreading through the plain,
If you can see great things in small beginnings
  And humble saints rule empires yet unseen,
If you can suffer and shout hallelujah,
  You have the faith to be a Nazarene.[1]

—Raymond Browning

But just as he who
called you is holy,
so be holy in all you do;
for it is written:
"Be holy,
because I am holy."
—1 Pet. 1:15-16 (NIV)

1 ❈ "Take Time to Be Holy"
God's Plan for a Satisfying Life

Being holy takes time. It first takes time for the thoughtful seeking and soul-deep consideration of God's offer of holy wholeness.

To be holy takes time because it requires heart searching, facing the subtle vice grip of carnality, a wholesale sell-out of self to God, an exposure to the demands and promises of biblical teaching, and a faith that what is promised will be ours. It takes time to die to self-sovereignty and to admit a dark side of our personhood needs cleansing.

I love the way the life of holiness answers the songwriter's prayer, "Lord Jesus, I long to be perfectly whole" (STTL, 513). The song is based on Paul's compelling benediction: "May God himself, the God of peace, sanctify you through and through. May your whole spirit, soul and body be kept blameless at the coming of our Lord Jesus Christ" (1 Thess. 5:23, NIV). "Through and through . . . your whole spirit, soul and body"—that means the whole person is kept blameless.

It takes time to recognize the need to be sanctified holy. And after the epic moment when the fullness is received, it takes time to live out this holy relationship with God.

Of course, being holy takes time. But many Nazarene pioneers commended the search and rejoiced in the result. The resulting life of love is essentially the kind of living that God intended for the human family before the sinful fall of our first parents.

Let's listen to Nazarene leaders of previous generations describe their joyful discovery.

—Neil B. Wiseman

The Tread of a Conqueror to Holiness

I know that we are a small company of the great army of our King, but I would not forget that we are picked people on special duty. We are a small detached force, called by God for special and most important work. We are especially commissioned to uphold the banner of holiness and to charge the enemy with the power of the Blood. Our work for the time may be comparatively local, but your flashing blades have been seen throughout the land, and if faithful, the light of your spears will reach to the ends of the earth.

You are called to lift high the banner of holiness, to preach *the* blessing of Christ and lead men and women into its fullness, to do this unencumbered by the hindrances that come to most who would seek the same ends. God has cut us loose from old traditions and heavy camp equipage and armed us for the fight.

God has called us to most heroic service. We are to be a band like Gideon's. God said in choosing us, "If there be any attractions that can draw you away, go now." If old associations or tastes or ease or respectability are likely to affect you, you are not really of this company. If you do not so hear the call of God that you cannot well be anywhere else, you have not fully the spirit of this work. It is not simply a call by preference for a church. It is the call of God to proclaim holiness, without compromise or hindrance.

This work means being filled with an intensity and enthusiasm that overmasters natural tastes, desires, and conveniences; that does not wait to drink, but lifts a little water in the hand to wet the lips while running to accomplish the work commissioned.[1]

—Phineas F. Bresee
1838—1915
Founding General Superintendent

The Possibilities of Being Spiritual

I want to go deeper before I go farther, and as I go farther, I must become more and more transformed into the likeness of God by worshiping Him more fully and more constantly.

I want to come to the place where things spiritual will mean more and more in my life. I want to worship God more supremely. I want to love the Church more unselfishly. I want to seek the salvation of souls more insistently. I want to bear the disagreeable more uncomplainingly. I want to be more deeply thankful for favors shown me by men and God.

And I am encouraged. I believe that God is going to help me on toward my heart's desire. In fact, I am sure God is helping me now. I may not be able to discern a great deal of difference just by tomorrow, but within a week or a month or a year—or somewhere down the line of life and duty—I am confident that I will find myself rewarded by fuller and deeper life in the Spirit. I shall become more spiritual by continually choosing to be so and by exercising myself unceasingly to reach that end. Just as we learn to do by doing, so shall we be by striving to become. "Lord, make me more like Thee."[2]

—J. B. Chapman
1884—1947
Editor and General Superintendent

Holiness Is an Exciting Adventure

I once heard a minister say, "We mustn't try to dramatize the religion of Jesus Christ." But after he said that, my mind went off on an adventure. I saw the leaves of history blow back and back . . . and there was a curtain of fire swirling up on the most dramatic scene in the record of things. There was fire all over the place. There were voices and excitement and wonder. A fisherman was flinging thunder down on a startled international crowd, saying, "This is that which was prophesied by the prophet Joel . . ."

Take it from there. Drama? My soul. The chronology of early Christianity is dramatic. The Acts of the Apostles. There is no more dramatic book in all the libraries of the earth, fact or fiction. There's nothing cool and static about that book. You can't peruse it with mathematical equations in your cranium. There is bugle song and power. There is the sound of gales blasting the shattered masts of ships, and the sound of stubborn, ragged sandals tramping through Asiatic dust. And, always, there is fire. Fire, and miracles, and singing. Drama? Aye, drama enough to shake a man's soul to its depths.

Every great spiritual revival of the Christian religion was a mighty drama in history. There is quick-tongued Luther and the great-minded Wesley. There is the dramatic cry of penitent sinners and the shout of converted sinners. There is fire. There is music. There is drumstir and the cry of horns. Christianity is life. And life is dramatic.[3]

—Lon Woodrum
1901-95
Evangelist

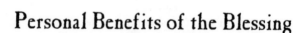

Personal Benefits of the Blessing

Theories of holiness may be proved logically, philosophically, and psychologically. But I should like to tell what the blessing of heart holiness means to me.

The hunger, the ache, the thirsting for something from some source was gone. The very first meal in Beulah was so satisfying as to fill my starving spirit with the delightful portions of health and joy of soul.

Holiness is to me a rest-producing blessing. As Israel rested in the Promised Land with the tiresome wilderness wanderings forever behind them, so my poor soul relaxed in the joy of His holy presence. With rapture today, my soul remembers that happy day when He came in Pentecostal fullness. The blazing glory of that hour has passed, but the *rest* remains. The first burst of uncontainable joy has passed, but the stability of that Presence is mine.[4]

—Lawrence B. Hicks
1913-75
Pastor and District Superintendent

The Incredible Possibilities of Holiness

God makes it possible that all the Christian graces may grow and develop unhindered in the sanctified soul. A fertile vineyard kept perfectly clean from all hindering growths, well cultivated with plenty of moisture and sunshine will produce the greatest possible amount of fruit. Just so with the vineyard of the soul and therefore He purgeth it that it may "[bring] forth [more and] much fruit" (John 15:5) and be continuous in its fruitfulness, "[bearing] twelve manner [crops] of fruits and [yielding] her fruit every month" (Rev. 22:2). Holiness is not a finished product, but a continuous process of development. It is a life's business of momentary trust and unshaken faith in God for all our needs, both temporal and spiritual, and will mould and develop holy Christian character that will stand forever. We are building for eternity, therefore we must build upon the only sure foundation, *the Rock of Ages,* and must build according to the pattern that Jesus has left us, "Holiness unto the Lord."[5]

—Theodore Ludwig
1871—1957
Evangelist

Impossibilities in a Holy Christian

It is impossible for pride and humility to live under the same skin.

It is impossible for you to be a teacher if you are unwilling to be taught.

It is impossible for you to be a leader if you are not willing to be led.

It is impossible for you to be a commander if you are not willing to obey.

It is impossible for a man to climb Zion's hill carrying a load of conceit.

It is impossible for a man to be any better on the outside than he is on the inside.

It is impossible for a man to walk straight if he lives a crooked life.

It is impossible for a man to succeed in life if he spends his spare time sitting on a goods box and chewing Star Navy, talking about how the government ought to be run.

It is impossible for a man with a level head, a clean heart, a big soul, a good experience, and a loving disposition to fail.[6]

—Bud Robinson
1860–1942
Evangelist

<hr>

Holiness—the Nazarene Message of Full Salvation

The Nazarene message is a message of full salvation. We must never swerve from the main issue—that of "holiness." However good or important, nothing can be placed on an equality with this great doctrine and experience—without which "no man shall see the Lord" (Heb. 12:14).

The apostle Paul in his advice to Timothy writes, "The end of the commandment is charity out of a pure heart, and of a good conscience, and of faith unfeigned: from which some having swerved have turned aside unto vain jangling; desiring to be teachers of the law" (1 Tim. 1:5-7).

When the spirituality of a church begins to decline, the wheels of ecclesiasticism begin to multiply. In proportion as people fall from grace, and turn aside from the great purpose of the commandment, they begin to magnify law, legal procedure, and technicalities. Invariably they fall into vain jangling over minor and nonessential things.

Paul said of the law teachers of his day that they understood not what they said, nor whereof they affirmed, and observation leads us to believe that this class has made little advance since that time.[7]

—H. Orton Wiley
1877—1961
Theologian and College President

The Connection Between Holiness and Heaven

That holiness and heaven have more in common than the first letter of each word is just as certain as anything can be. Heaven is a holy place, into which shall never enter anything that defiles or is unclean.

Because this is true, Christians in all ages and in all denominations have agreed that before human beings can enter a holy heaven they must themselves be holy. Theories as to the how, the when, and the where of it are many and varied. But there is no argument about the requirement.

Some will have it that holiness is by growth. Others claim that holiness is by death. While strictly speaking the Catholic purgatory is not related to the problem of inbred sin, yet it is supposed to complete the preparation of the soul for the holiness of heaven.

Without pausing to examine these alternative views, we may note a very different emphasis in the New Testament. It shows up clearly in the high-priestly prayer of Jesus in John 17. This was a prayer not only for the disciples there present "but for them also which shall believe on me through their word" (v. 20).

Jesus said, "I pray not that thou shouldest take them out of the world, but that thou shouldest keep them from the evil" (v. 15). The Kingdom had greater need of witnesses on earth than jewels in heaven.

Yet the prayer in verse 17, "Sanctify them," had the ring of urgency in it. In the present experience of sanctifying grace, the disciples in all ages are to be kept from evil while still in the world.[8]

—W. T. Purkiser
1910-92
Editor and College President

Holiness Is a Central Issue

When holiness is a personal heart experience, the entire thought and words and life become permeated and saturated, so that holiness no longer is merely a luxurious privilege, or perchance a side issue, or an addendum to the book; no, holiness now fills the horizon of the thought life.

Our God is a specialist on holiness. The objective of every blessing and of every commandment, and of every promise pertaining to redemption, is our deliverance from sin, and restoration to holiness.[9]

—C. W. Ruth
1865—1941
Associate Pastor to Bresee

Holy and Human Too!

Near the beginning of *Pilgrim's Progress* there is an interesting conversation. Overburdened Christian had met Evangelist and had asked for help and direction. Evangelist pointed into the distance and asked, "Do you see yon wicket gate?" Christian looked and honestly answered, "No." Then Evangelist, trying again, said, "Do you see yonder shining light?" Christian strained his eyes and saw one spot that seemed less dark than the rest and answered, "I think I do." "Then keep that light in your eye," said Evangelist, "and go directly thereto, so shalt thou see the gate."

There are personal problems that are confusing, and oftentimes we almost lose sight of the "wicket gate." But there is a way out; and thus we have hope for tomorrow. We must confess that we have not found all the answers. We do not understand the full meaning of our complex personalities; we do not know the geography of all our moods and temperaments.

Even with a definite transformation and being a real sanctified Christian, you will likely discover you're human too! In these moments, discouragement is a weapon used by the enemy to drag the child of God down to defeat. But that is the time to trust. We walk by faith a great deal of the way toward the city of God.[10]

—J. E. Williams
d. 1968
Pastor

What Is Consecration?

If we are going to know anything about excellency in life, we must give ourselves in consecration to one field, making everything else to serve this which we have chosen to be primary. Christian consecration is not a choice primarily between good and evil but a matter of making God first and therefore everything else secondary.

We have wrapped up in our idea of Christian holiness so much that is unreal. We have been wrong. Consecration is just as real and is just as normal and is just as vital as any other choice or decision of life. It is simply a matter of making God and the will of God forever first in life.[11]

—Orval J. Nease
1891—1950
General Superintendent

Consecration Means Giving Oneself Away to God's Purpose

In Acts 2:17, "last days" includes all the days of the gospel age from the descent of the Holy Spirit on the Day of Pentecost until "the Lord himself shall descend from heaven with a shout, with the voice of the archangel, and with the trump of God" (1 Thess. 4:16).

The Holy Spirit came to make Christians adequate to meet the demands of their generation. The history of the victorious Church is in fact the biography of Spirit-filled persons. Where there has been failure, it has been because persons have not opened their hearts to the incoming of the Holy Spirit. They have depended upon their resources and their skills rather than on the Spirit of God who had been promised by the Father.

In this age we all stand amazed at the marvels that have been done because the atom has been split and nuclear energy has been released. The spiritual equivalent is in the power of the Spirit. To all who will come to God with openness to receive and readiness to be used, the gift of the Holy Spirit will be bestowed. None can manipulate the Spirit of God to do their will. But they can yield themselves to the Spirit to perform God's will. The maximum accomplishment in the work of God is by total yieldedness to the control of the Spirit. By giving His wisdom, believers understand what the will of God is; and in His power the work is done.[12]

—G. B. Williamson
1898—1981
General Superintendent

Holiness Requires a Crucifixion

"I have been crucified with Christ and I no longer live, but Christ lives in me. The life I live in the body, I live by faith in the Son of God, who loved me and gave himself for me" (Gal. 2:20,

NIV). "The fruit of the Spirit is love, joy, peace, patience, kindness, goodness, faithfulness, gentleness and self-control" (5:22-23, NIV).

Self-crucifixion must replace self-coronation, or the fruit of the Spirit will remain only a dream but never a reality. *sermon* 3/9/08

Every resurrection must be preceded by a crucifixion. You can't come to Easter Sunday without going through Good Friday. That's a chronological fact, but it has personal-experience realities. You can't reach the empty tomb unless you take the road that goes through the Garden of Gethsemane and past the cross of Calvary. One of the great paradoxes of Christianity is simply this: You have to die to live.

George Mueller, that great man of faith in Bristol, England, said, "There was a day when I died, utterly died." And on his 90th birthday he wrote these words: "I was converted in November 1825, but I only came into the full surrender of the heart four years later, in July 1829. The love of money was gone; the love of place was gone; God, God alone, became my portion." George Mueller also said, "After I was filled with the Spirit, I learned more about the Scriptures in four hours than I had learned in the previous four years."

Jesus said, "If anyone would come after me, he must deny himself and take up his cross [that's self-crucifixion] and follow me." Then He went on to say, "Whoever loses his life for me will find it" (Matt. 16:24-25, NIV).

We sing, "Let me lose myself and find it, Lord, in Thee." The song underscores a profound truth. You cannot really find your true self, your "Christed" self, unless and until you lose your false self, your carnal self, through full commitment to Christ.[13]

—Ralph Earle
1907-95
Seminary Professor

Jesus—Our Pattern for a Holy Life

Christianity is a religion of self-denial. Its Founder taught that if we would be His true disciples, we must deny ourselves and take up our cross daily and follow Him. For he that will save his life shall lose it. And He has given us an example that we should follow in His steps. His whole life, His suffering, His death—all was in self-abnegation and devotion to others. He was not a helpless martyr. He emptied himself, that He might fill others. He beggared himself, that He might enrich others. He said: "Therefore doth my Father love me, because I lay down my life. . . . No man taketh it from me, but I lay it down of myself. I have power to lay it down, and I have power to take it again. This commandment have I received of my Father" (John 10:17-18).

The disciples to a man promised to stand by their Lord. Yet when the testing time came, they all forsook Him and fled. Thus they illustrated the human desire for self-preservation. It takes holiness—wholeness of devotion to God—to make one willing to give his blood as the seed of the Church.

Jesus foresaw that those disciples would fail in testing. He knew that they would stumble because of Him that night. He would save them from further failure. Therefore in His prayer He said, "And for their sakes I sanctify myself [sacrifice, devote myself, in utter self-denial], that they also might be [truly] sanctified" (17:19).[14]

—E. F. Walker
1852—1918
General Superintendent

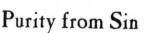

Purity from Sin

I once sat in a great London church and heard the pastor preach a smart, modernist sermon in which he called sin "a mere peccadillo"—"a slight offense"—"a petty fault."

Poor silly misinformed preacher. Sin is rebellion against

God. Sin is lawlessness. Sin is the monkey wrench thrown with malicious hand into the delicate moral machinery of God's universe. It is the most dangerous thing in the whole world. And the preacher who does not know this is as brainless as the chattering monkey from which he thinks he has descended.

Reason has given us clear vision to see that we are in a universe of law. Planets and suns circle around their controlling centers, held to an unchanging orbit by an invisible chain of law. The chemical elements in the material world around us have fixed methods of action and combination in which every atom is obedient. Fire will burn; water will drown; poison will kill. Disobey or disrespect the nature of these elements and we shall suffer the painful or fatal consequences.

Unperverted moral reason tells us it is precisely so with sin. It affirms that all sin is a transgression of divine law, and there follows in its train a swift disaster. It is as if a planet should fall in its train or stray from its orbit and go wandering through space—without the guiding hand of God.[15]

—A. M. Hills
1848–1951
Theologian and College President

"Lord, Send the Fire!"

The prophet Elijah was not afraid of fire. On Mount Carmel he had to deal with the prophets of Baal. The battle waxed hot, but Elijah was not to be defeated. He called for a showdown. He declared that the God that answered by fire should be worshiped as God. He let the idol worshipers lead off. They prepared the sacrifice and with much vehemence called on their gods—but no fire fell. They failed and that miserably.

Then it was Elijah's turn. He prepared his sacrifice and soaked it with water. He wanted to convince the crowd beyond any doubt. When everything was in perfect readiness, the old prophet stepped back, raised his hands toward heaven, and called on God to send the fire. The result was awe inspiring and most encouraging to Elijah. The fire consumed the sacrifice, melted the stones, and dried up the water that filled the trenches about the altar. What a victory for God and Elijah. Elijah believed in the supernatural.

When the Holy Ghost dispensation was ushered in on the morning of that first Christian Pentecost, there was the element of fire. "And there appeared unto them cloven tongues like as of fire, and it sat upon each of them" (Acts 2:3).

Fire accompanies the baptism of the Holy Ghost. It is the fire that purges, purifies, and makes clean the temple so that it becomes a fit place for the Holy Ghost to abide. It is the fire that burns out the dross. It is the fire that saves us from indifference, carelessness, lukewarmness, and spiritual dry rot.

It is the fire that energizes and puts a spiritual drive in the soul. It is the fire that eliminates the fear of man and makes it easy to witness for Christ. It is the fire that burns the purse strings and makes it easy to bring in our tithes and make offerings so that the kingdom of God can be advanced and the gospel carried to the uttermost parts of the earth.

It is the fire that keeps us spiritually hot within and gives us that inner adornment "which is in the sight of God of great price" (1 Pet. 3:4).[16]

—C. Warren Jones
1882—1963
Secretary of World Missions

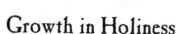

Growth in Holiness
Starts with a Pure Heart

The soul satisfied in God will make progress in the knowledge of the things of God. The suggestion made by some that if sin were destroyed within the soul, there would then be neither room for growth nor incentive to it is as thoughtless as it is false.

What, we ask, is the foundation of true growth? The answer surely is obvious: growth is facilitated by constitutional soundness. The child, the plant, the lamb, the sapling, the ripening fruit—surely none of these require an inner corruption in order that a reasonable development might take place.

On the contrary, it is that very corruption, where there, that arrests development. The sick child weakens instead of growing strong. The diseased fruit rots instead of going on to ripen. The worm-eaten tree does not flourish; it quickly decays. Likewise the sin-infested soul does not and cannot develop as it should. Sin is not conducive to spiritual growth; it never was and never will be.[17]

—Harry E. Jessop
1884—1974
Writer and Evangelist

The Magnetic Power of Purity

Heart purity always issues in and is maintained by a glad embracing of the Father's will, whatever it may be.

Brengle dictated these moving words to his wife during one of his most serious illnesses: "I think there is a noble majesty in pain. It is pleasure strung to concert pitch. A great musician can discover harmonies where an ordinary fellow could hear only discords: and I seem to sense that there is, somehow or somewhere, to be discovered a great harmony in pain."

Harmony in pain. Dictated from a sickbed. A thoughtful Christian in a reflective mood can pen such thoughts in his study, but only a saint can dictate them from a bed of weakness and pain. Sanctification enables us to kiss the will of God whatever mask it wears.[18]

—Jack Ford
1908-74
British Pastor

cpy

Purity and Power Belong Together

Purity means power. Not power to be strange, but power to do common things in a supernatural way. Not a power to lead a spectacular life, but a *holy* one—a life that is divinely natural, not marred by the unnaturalness of sin and inner defeat. Power to endure, to love, and to believe.

It may not be a limelight power, but it is sure to be a field or shop or laundry room or kitchen power that glorifies God most by resting on the humblest and most unlikely believer. Nor is it a power to escape being tempted, but to escape *when* tempted. Nor is it, always, a power to carry out one's plans successfully, but a power to see them smashed into hopeless bits without despairing or becoming resentful. Nor is it a power to gather possessions, but a power to lose them without losing joy, contentment, and faith.

This is the kind of power we need. And though we search the religions of all lands and examine all the cults, creeds, and religious fads in the world, we will never find it apart from the personal, instantaneous experience of heart cleansing provided by the blood of Jesus Christ and accomplished by the baptism with the Holy Ghost.[19]

—Richard S. Taylor
1912-
Theologian and Seminary Professor

The Power of Holy Love at Work

God speaks in no other way as He does through human lips. The divinest power manifested in this universe is the love of God out of a pure heart, spoken through pure lips, melting the heart of a sinner and lifting a lost soul from the very brink of hell. God manifested in the flesh, speaking through lips of clay, is the password to victory.[20]

—Phineas F. Bresee
1838—1915
Founding General Superintendent

The Enabling Provision of the Holy Spirit

Every individual human being seeks power. No one is so humble, so inarticulate, so inadequate, but seeks to find in himself some evidence of superiority over his fellows. What price men have paid, throughout the ages, for the possession of power. So, the disciples of Jesus. True, He had sent them forth with power over sickness, even with power over demons, and they had returned rejoicing. But the power to bless was not especially in their thinking when the Master promised them the power of the Holy Ghost coming upon them.

Again and again they had sought Him for position power in His kingdom—meaning prominence in earthly rulership. At last, Jesus turning to them, reminded them of His promise of the baptism with the Holy Ghost—the baptism of Jesus—calling their attention to John's distinguishing evaluation of the baptism with water and baptism with the Spirit. It is the coming of this latter baptism, Jesus tells them, that will fill them with power.

They were to have power over sin—the power of indwelling holiness—carnality having been burned out in the fiery baptism with the Spirit. Then, as a consequence of that cleansing, and the filling with the Divine Personality, they were to have power to witness for Jesus to the uttermost parts of the earth.[21]

—Charles A. McConnell
1860–1955
Pastor

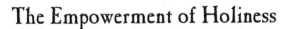

The Empowerment of Holiness

Traveling along the highway, one can often see coils of wire waiting to be strung up on the poles. Here will be two or three huge coils; then a half mile father on there will be more coils. Just disconnected coils of wire—of no use to anyone. But when the workmen come along and fuse those wires together and then connect them with the dynamos and with the outlets where the electricity is to be used, those wires become useful—conductors of energy and power. And only as the connections are made at *both* ends are the wires channels of a current.

Congregations are like that. Some congregations are nothing but a collection of disconnected coils—no power there, no energy there. Only when they are fused together by the flame of God's Holy Spirit and then "connected" to the dynamos of God's power *and* the outlets of needy souls—only then are they useful and powerful and conductors of the redeeming current of God's love.

Let us ever remember, however, that *we* are not the power. *We* are not the energy. We are but the *conductors* of that energy. We are but the *channels* of that power![22]

—C. William Fisher
1916-
Evangelist

Faith Required to Maintain Holiness

It requires just as much faith to retain the experience of holiness as it did to obtain it. Faith is not simply an act, but an attitude; that we must believe, and then keep right on believing, "for by faith ye stand" (2 Cor. 1:24). "Without faith it is impossible to please him" (Heb. 11:6). He who lays aside his faith and depends on his feelings, or seeks to rest in the fact that he was sanctified some time in the past, is almost certain to become a seeker in the next revival because of his doubts and uncertainty. We can retain the experience only as we "are kept by the power of God through faith" (1 Pet. 1:5).

However, in the continued exercise of a lively faith we may reach the persuasion the apostle Paul had reached when he said, "I know whom I have believed, and am persuaded that he is able to keep that which I have committed unto him against that day." "I am persuaded, that neither death, nor life, nor angels, nor principalities, nor powers, nor things present, nor things to come, nor height, nor depth, nor any other creature, shall be able to separate us from the love of God, which is in Christ Jesus our Lord" (2 Tim. 1:12; Rom. 8:38-39).

Holiness requires a present tense faith for a present tense victory. Jesus is ever saying, "According to your faith be it unto you" (Matt. 9:29). Hence the apostle said, while enumerating the Christian's armor, "Above all, taking the shield of faith, wherewith ye shall be able to quench all the fiery darts of the wicked" (Eph. 6:16). However bright the experience of the past it will not keep itself; nor can it be retained by resting in said experience and a faltering faith. "We walk by faith" (2 Cor. 5:7).[23]

—C. W. Ruth
1865—1941
Associate Pastor to Bresee

Self-Crucified with Christ

We are face-to-face with the assertion that you lose something before you gain the heart's desire and meet life's demand. Well, Peter deserted that night, and all the rest retreated in confusion and disappointment; but we shall not. We must see it through. How much is revealed to us about ourselves as we watch His trial and agony. And then we are driven out of the city by the crowd as it rejects Him and sends Him to the hill and four crosses. Yes, four—one for Him, two for the thieves, and one that is empty, which He indicates is for us. "No, not death, it is life that I want," I cry. But He replies that whoever will not suffer with Him will not reign with Him. And so, I face the cross.

We cannot be what we want without facing the cross. We must die out to self and sin. As completely as we know how, we must join our Master in saying, "Not my will, but thine, be done" (Luke 22:42). The death of the cross is not a sudden affair, I fear. Though it may occupy only a few minutes or seconds, it involves a lifetime. It means the constant facing up to God's "What else?" until we have gone through every excuse and subterfuge and are emptied of every sin and human purpose for life before Him, in the light of His holy will. It means the journey into the depth until nothing remains but a complete and unreserved surrender to the highest, holiest, and best.

There are some who have done this and have looked up at last to say, "All right, I have done all that I know to do, and yet nothing has happened." As though the Master expected it, He replies, "Tarry ye in the city of Jerusalem, until ye be endued with power from on high" (Luke 24:49). For the surrendered life may know the joy of Easter morning and yet have much dialogue in the ensuing days with the Master at the place of crucifixion until the Holy Spirit fully comes. And it is Pentecost, and not Easter, that makes the man of God a power in the world. Now please understand me; I do not mean that Easter is unimportant in Christian experience. Rather, it is that Easter finds its demonstration in the power of Pentecost.

We find new life in dying and being raised with Christ. But the double portion of the Spirit of Christ comes to us in the personal Pentecost that awaits every believer, and without which we are less than the persons our times demand.[24]

—Ted E. Martin
1911-97
Pastor

The Bible Teaches a Second Work of Grace

A seeker ready to be convinced by the authority of the Bible wrote to the editor of the *Herald of Holiness* (now *Holiness Today*): "Would you please either publish or send me some Scripture references that verify our belief in the baptism with the Holy Spirit and sanctification as a second definite work of grace?"

This is a large order, but here are a few:

Matt. 3:11-12—The baptism with the Spirit *follows* water baptism.

Matt. 5:48—These words are addressed to those who are *Christians* (God is their Heavenly Father).

Luke 11:13—The Holy Spirit is given to those who come to God *as their Heavenly Father*.

John 14:15-18—The world cannot receive the Holy Spirit. The *disciples* can and shall.

John 17:17—Christ prays for His *disciples* to be sanctified (see vv. 3-16).

Acts 2:1-4—All so filled with the Spirit were *disciples* of the Lord.

Acts 8:5-17—The Samaritans were *baptized believers* before they were filled with the Spirit.

Acts 19:5-6—The disciples at Ephesus were baptized with water by Paul, and *after that* were filled with the Spirit.

Rom. 6:6, 11, 22; 8:2-4, 6-9—Freedom from inner sin is promised to *Christians*.

Rom. 12:12—Consecration is a *Christian* obligation.

2 Cor. 7:1—*Christians* are to be cleansed to perfect holiness.

Eph. 4:20-24—*Christians* are to put off the "old man."

Eph. 5:18—The command to "be filled with the Spirit" is given to believers.

Eph. 5:25-27—Christ gave himself to "sanctify and cleanse" *the Church*.

1 Thess. 4:3, 7-8; 5:23-24—*Christians* are called to holiness, to be sanctified wholly.

Titus 2:11-14—The grace of God provides not only *redemption* but *purity*.

Heb. 6:1-3—*Believers* must "go on unto perfection."

Heb. 12:14-16—Holiness is essential to "see the Lord" and *to prevent backsliding*.

Heb. 13:12—Christ suffered to sanctify "*[his] people* with his own blood" (italics added).

James 4:8—Sinners are to cleanse their hands; the *double-minded,* to *purify* their hearts.

1 Pet. 1:14-16—God calls His *obedient children* to holiness in all manner of living.

1 John 1:7—Only *Christians* walk in the light, and as they do they are cleansed from all sin.

1 John 3:2-3—Those *with hope of seeing Christ* purify them-selves, even as He is pure.

The point of these references, as you see, is that they relate to those who are already converted. That what is to be done for them is a "definite work of grace" is seen in the use of such terms as "baptize," "make perfect," "receive" the Holy Spirit, "fill," "cleanse," "put off," "put on," and so on. None of these terms suggests a gradual process that goes on through all of life and is never finished until the hour of death. They rather speak of what has a definite beginning in the experience of the believer, although its effects continue through all of life.[25]

—W. T. Purkiser
1910-92
Editor and Professor

2 ❊ "Speak Oft with Thy Lord"
Prayer—Mysterious Relationship with the Helper

———— ⊷✠⊶ ————

Trying to understand prayer can be difficult. We question why the creative, redeeming, holy God has interest or patience in hearing from us. We wonder how our conversation with God can make a difference. But that's what Scripture promises.

Maybe prayer should be viewed as being something like gravity. Though I understand almost nothing about how gravity works, it supports and sustains me every moment of every day.

From a different though noble perspective, God planned prayer to be a delight rather than a duty. How amazing—the King of Kings welcomes us into His throne room. He honors us by listening carefully to our petitions. No other experience in all the universe faintly compares with the worthless beggar being welcomed into such a lofty relationship to express his or her needs and to receive the assurance of life-transforming answers.

Prayer, especially practicing the Presence kind, provides a perennial freshness with God. I owe E. Stanley Jones thanks for that delightfully descriptive phrase.

Our foreparents believed the holy life was dependent on serious intercessory prayer that makes us comfortable in the presence of Jesus. They prayed. They recommended prayer. They received answers. For them, prayer was relationship with the Holy Helper—the living, giving Spirit of God. And they advise their spiritual descendants to pray too.

—Neil B. Wiseman

Prayer Is Risky Business

Prayer is more than our own sublime desire; it is an exposure to God that probes our soul to the very quick.

Think of it, audience with God. Risky business, frightening thought, that a man should come before the presence of the Judge of all the earth and there express his thoughts and desires. Someone has said, "God is a disturbing Person to meet." True enough, when we reflect that He sees through us when we pray. There can be no "front" or "parlor manners" with Him. The "psychological approach" will not impress Him. We have to come just as we are, for that is how He sees us. Sunday piety or prayer-time devotions will not do.[1]

—Samuel Young
1901-90
General Superintendent

Prayer and Faith Belong Together

Prayer! Here is the problem. There is little faith because there is little prayer. Prayer and faith are like Siamese twins joined at the heart—separate them and both die. When we don't pray, we can't say, "Rise up and walk." We can only say, "Sit there and die." Or, "Move over, I'll flop down and die with you."[2]

—William E. McCumber
1927-
Pastor and Editor

Pray and Faint Not

Why pray? Because we need to keep the wires clear between our souls and heaven. We are citizens of heaven who live surrounded by traitors and enemies; we dare not cut ourselves off from headquarters. "Prayer is keeping an appointment with God," giving Him an opportunity to get His special message through to us.

Why pray? Because through prayer we discern the will of God. Prayer is not all talking; a large share of it is listening. "Speak, LORD; for thy servant heareth" (1 Sam. 3:9). So we shall escape many mistakes and the emptiness of a helter-skelter, aimless life.

Why pray? Because prayer makes us better persons. We cannot come into God's holy presence honestly without putting sin out of our lives; we cannot come under the scrutiny of His clear eye without a cleansing of our thoughts and motives. We cannot ask forgiveness of our trespasses without forgiving others. We cannot seek His will as it is in heaven without becoming better adjusted, stronger, and steadier.

Why pray? Because through prayer we can invest in values that last. By prayer we little people can share the fruits and the rewards of the great soul winners. By prayer we can spread the Kingdom in lands that we shall never see. Prayer piles up compound interest.[3]

—Bertha Munro
1887—1983
Educator

The Wonder of Relationship with God

Paul, the prisoner of the Lord, bound in chains to a Roman guard, was on his knees in prayer. On his lips was the name of a city in another part of the world—Colossae. But Paul was not interested in geography; it was people who were on his heart, God's people. Oh, "that [they] might walk worthy of the Lord . . . fruitful in every good work; . . . strengthened with all might" (Col. 1:10).

How would God work to answer this prayer? What would be the process? Something of the answer is hinted in Paul's prayer— "that ye might be filled with the knowledge of his will in all wisdom and spiritual understanding; . . . increasing in the knowledge of God" (vv. 9-10).

A growing, intimate, loving, personal acquaintance with God himself, that is the foundation of growth in grace. Emotions, ecstasies, raptures, elations—these are thrilling but passing. But to have the wonder and reality of God grow on one day by day, that is spiritual life and power.[4]

—Roy E. Swim
1899—1992
Children's Editor

God's Guide for Holy Living

The great revival at Pentecost was followed by remarkable results and set a standard for genuine Pentecostal work in all ages.

"They . . . received [the] word [gladly]" (Acts 2:41). The record states that about 3,000 souls received the Word with gladness. It is a fact that the manner in which a soul receives the Word of God determines largely his future attitude toward that Word. There is a gladness related to the gospel of Christ, and it was this gladness that formed the strength of the Early Church and should be the source of its power today.

"They continued steadfastly" (v. 42). The after results of this revival were a continuation of that which happened during the revival. There was a gracious steadfastness in the converts that seems to be sadly lacking today. The new converts were at once baptized and gladly entered into all the spiritual activities of the Church. They seemed to have a desire for things spiritual.

"In the apostles' doctrine" (v. 42). The evangelistic preaching had enough doctrine in it to furnish the converts with a knowledge of the duties of the Christian life, which they put in practice after the revival was over. Doctrine is only cold and dead because the preacher is. Doctrine furnishes the bullets and not the powder. The evangelist is to preach sound doctrine with the Holy Ghost sent down from heaven. Doctrine is the King's great highway over which we are to travel to the holy city. We need sound doctrine set on fire with divine passion that will leave its mark on new converts; doctrine that will start them toward heaven and a life of usefulness in the Church.[5]

—N. B. Herrell
1877—1953
Evangelist

Stewardship of Prayer

Prayer is power. It changes things. By means of prayer mixed with faith, the very thunderbolts of Deity are laid at the sanctified believer's feet. He is bidden to hurl them, with praying breath, into problems for their solving; in the sin situation for its cleansing; into wrongs that tower like mountains, for their moving; into distresses standing like sycamine trees, for their uprooting.

Prayer is dynamic. "And nothing shall be impossible" (Matt. 17:20) to the praying believer. "And all things, whatsoever ye shall ask in prayer, believing, ye shall receive" (21:22). How startling! How saturated with Deity! How limitless!

And all this power, this dynamite, this limitless spiritual force is handed to us, His children. We are bidden to be molders of men's lives, of the future of churches, of the character of denominations, of the trend of nations, of the outcome of elections, of the salvation of the heathen, of the destiny of the ages.[6]

—J. G. Morrison
1871—1939
General Secretary of World Missions

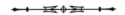

The Hidden Becomes Visible

To begin to recognize that the intangible world is indeed the deepest reality, one must begin to remember that values, honesty, faith, love, trust, hope, dignity, purpose, character (none of which can ever be seen with our eyes or held in our hands) are the real realities of our lives. Their true realness can be seen in their power to mold us when they are embraced. And it may be seen just as surely from the emptiness that results when we disdain them.

Maybe we need to know, too, that the reality of the Kingdom is a discipline that can be learned. One must submit to its demands.

Tennis takes a racquet, a ball, shoes, a court, some skills, some energy, some aching muscles, some winning, some losing, and some recovery shots for match point after four hours in the afternoon sun. One doesn't get a racquet for his birthday and enter the U.S. Open. To get to know God also requires some time, some listening, some quiet, some discipline, some desire, however faltering our ways of hearing may seem to be at first.

The longing in our hearts is already the faint perception of the voice of God calling us. We could begin to acknowledge Him even if it were only to ask Him for some little thing that only He could give, some direction, some sense of purpose or inner help by which only we would know something had been accomplished. Maybe a simple "answer me if You are there" kind of prayer is what we need to pray.

So I guess I really want to answer the longing, haunting questions of my friend. Is there somebody on the other side of the net? Will the ball come bouncing back to me if I smash it across the net? If I throw prayers into the sky, will words come raining down around me?

With all my heart, I want to tell him that it is his serve. Go ahead and hit the ball. The silence will speak to you. The unseen will appear. The untouchable will grip you. The hidden will become visible. The unreachable can be reached.

God has something to say to you, and you can hear Him if you listen.[7]

—Bob Benson
1931-86
Speaker and Writer

How to Maintain Deep Spirituality

If George Mueller, the great apostle of faith in Bristol, England, needed every morning to wait upon God, reading his Bible until his heart was blessed and his soul afire with God's presence, however much more do the ordinary rank and file of people need to tarry daily for the manifestation of God's presence and glory. George Mueller took time to read the Bible and pray. He kept Christ first, through the medium of his intensified, systematic, devotional exercises.

Our devotions should never be allowed to become a mere mechanical exercise—so much Bible reading every day and so much time spent in prayer. We must learn to keep our souls blessed and in touch with God. Whether preacher or layman, we shall be tremendously helped and blessed if we will but spend one hour, or 30 minutes, or even less time before God in the study of the Word and prayer, if this time be spent in vital communion with God. We must exercise ourselves to keep a devotional frame of mind. We should guard our tongues. We should seek to live in a heavenly atmosphere and to keep our minds continually stayed on God. In other words, take time to pray and systematically study the Bible from a devotional standpoint. We have the privilege of tarrying before God until our souls are really blessed.[8]

—E. O. Chalfant
1887—1954
District Superintendent

The Prayer Jesus Refused to Pray

In the high-priestly prayer of our Lord (John 17) we find Jesus praying for many things for His disciples. He prayed for their keeping (vv. 11, 15), for their unity (vv. 11, 21, 23), for their joy (v. 13), for their sanctification (vv. 17, 19), for their perfection (v. 23), for their final salvation (v. 24), for them to see God's glory (v. 24), and for them to have God's love in them (v. 26).

However, at one point in His prayer, Jesus stopped: "I pray not that thou shouldest take them out of the world" (v. 15). It was the prayer Jesus refused to pray. He could have prayed for them to be translated to heaven with Him. He could have locked arms with them, all stepping up on heaven's cloud and ascending together. They would have missed all the stonings, beatings, imprisonments, persecutions, and brutal deaths for His name's sake. But Christ would not allow it. He would not even pray for it.

Why did Jesus refuse to pray this prayer? Why did He go back to the splendors of heaven and leave them in this world of woe? Two reasons. First, they needed to stay here for their own good. They needed the trials and persecutions to strengthen their moral fiber and make them stand tall in a sinful world. Second, they needed to stay here because the world needed them. The world was in darkness, and they were light. The world was rotting, and they were salt. The world was in despair, and they represented hope. The world was without God, and they had God to offer. The world needed to hear what they had to say.

But our Lord assumed a certain special responsibility toward His disciples when He refused their immediate deliverance from this world. He obligated himself to give them the grace of inner cleansing and power that would enable this tiny group to turn the world right side up. Therefore, Jesus prayed, "Sanctify them" (v. 17). And His prayer was answered (Acts 2:4). He also prayed this prayer for you (John 17:20). Has Christ's prayer for you been answered? It can be today.[9]

—**Fletcher Spruce**
1913-74
Pastor and District Superintendent

When God Taps You on the Shoulder

The late Peter Marshall, for years the young, dynamic pastor of the New York Avenue Presbyterian Church, Washington, D.C., and, until his untimely death at 46, chaplain of the United States Senate, asked a question that gets at the very heart of Christian living:

"If you were walking down the street, and someone came up behind you and tapped you on the shoulder—what would you do?"

Naturally, you would turn around.

Well, that is exactly what happens in the spiritual world.

A man walks through life, with the eternal call ringing in his ears but with no response stirring in his heart; and then suddenly, without any warning, the Spirit taps him on the shoulder.

What happens? He turns around. The word "repentance" means "turning around."

The tap on the shoulder is the call that brooks no refusal, the call we cannot ignore, the call that brings us to fall adoringly and wonderingly at the feet of Christ.

The supreme call, the one that penetrates deepest—down beneath the physical, the material, the monetary, the mental, and the social—to the very center of our innermost being, the quick of our soul—is the spiritual call from the voice of Christ. It is life's supreme moment.

When Jesus taps you on the shoulder in the midst of life's noise and rush and says, "The Master is come, and calleth for thee," your great hour of decision has arrived.

The tap on the shoulder stops you, His voice calls you, His love draws you, His kingdom challenges you. Now you must make a decision. You cannot be neutral. You must turn around and follow Him, or you deliberately walk on away from Him. Life is never the same after He taps you on the shoulder and speaks to your soul.[10]

—R. V. DeLong
1901-81
Educator and Radio Preacher

"I Thought I Was All Going to Skimmings"

When I sought to be sanctified, I had that strange, peculiar feeling that God was so close to me that my soul trembled in God's presence and it seemed that God kindled up a fire in the very bottom on my heart.

The only way that I can describe the feeling is that anger boiled up, and God skimmed it off. Pride boiled up, and God skimmed it off. Jealousy boiled up, and God skimmed it off. Envy boiled up, and God skimmed it off, until it seemed to me I was all going to skimmings.

I said, "Lord, there won't be anything left of me."

God seemed to say, "There will not be much left, but what little there is will be clean."

When my heart was emptied, then it seemed that a river of peace broke loose in the clouds. It was as sweet as honey and the honeycomb. It flowed into my empty heart until a few minutes later my heart was full and overflowing, and the waves of heaven became so great and grand and glorious that it seemed to me I would die if God did not stay His hand.

How little we know about the fullness of God and the greatness of God's power. Not half an hour before God cleansed me and filled me, I had told the Lord that I wanted Him to come with all the power that He had and sanctify me. Then I had told the Lord that very morning that I had read in His Book that if I would bring all the tithes into the storehouse and prove Him, He would open the windows of heaven and pour me out a blessing that there would not be room enough to receive it. Out of a hungry heart I had said, "O Lord, You cannot satisfy me with the windows of heaven; You will have to open the doors of heaven to pour out a blessing big enough to satisfy my hungry heart and soul." But, beloved, I did not know how large God's windows were and how small my heart was. God had never used that language but one time before, and at that time God opened the windows of heaven and poured out a flood on the earth. If God's windows are so large that He can pour out a flood through them, then you can see at a glance that God's windows are large enough to pour out a blessing into the heart of one of His believing children to the extent that he cannot receive but little of it. As the waves of heaven rolled over my soul, I finally got down on the ground and stretched out and, as wave after wave of glory rolled over me, told the Lord that if He didn't hold up a bit, there would be a dead man in the cornfield.[11]

—Bud Robinson
1860—1942
Evangelist

Abide in me,
and I in you.
As the branch cannot
bear fruit of itself,
except it abide in the vine;
no more can ye,
except ye abide in me.
—John 15:4

3 ❧ "Abide in Him Always"
The Holy Spirit—God in the Present Tense

I remember it well. We sang the song often in the little Church of the Nazarene on the east side of Detroit where I found faith. "He is with me ev'rywhere, / And He knows my ev'ry care. / I'm as happy as a bird and just as free: / For the Spirit has control; / Jesus satisfies my soul, / Since the Comforter abides with me" (STTL, 315).

Abiding on the human side is a will set to do God's will—no second thoughts, no negotiations, no deals, no discounts. On our Father's part, abiding is the truer-than-life assurance that the Holy Spirit is with us and has become the ever-present God for us. That means the life-giving Spirit is as near us as Jesus was near His disciples during His earthly ministry.

Consider these abiding passages from Scripture: (1) The abiding Christian does not sin—"Whosoever abideth in him sinneth not: whosoever sinneth hath not seen him, neither known him" (1 John 3:6). (2) The abiding Christian produces fruit—"As the branch cannot bear fruit of itself, except it abide in the vine; no more can ye, except ye abide in me" (John 15:4). And (3) the abiding Christian experiences answered prayer—"If ye abide in me, and my words abide in you, ye shall ask what ye will, and it shall be done unto you" (v. 7).

A friend who loves to preach on the abiding passages says abiding means to hang out with Jesus and, when all else fails, to "persevere—hang tough—hang in there." The history of the Church of the Nazarene has many witnesses to the benefits of persevering for God. Some descriptions of what they experienced follow.

—Neil B. Wiseman

Helps for Abiding from the Sanctuary

The Lord has promised to send us help from the sanctuary when we are in trouble. "The LORD hear thee in the day of trouble; . . . send thee help from the sanctuary" (Ps. 20:1-2).

There will never be any real substitute for church. We are admonished not to forsake "the assembling of ourselves together" (Heb. 10:25). Very few people ever backslide as long as they go to church twice on Sunday and on prayer meeting night.

The church must forever retain the soul-saving element in the services. There must be something that convicts and converts; a nice program is not enough. There must be straight gospel preaching. There should be such glorious singing as only sanctified people can do. Jesus said, "Ye are the salt of the earth: but if the salt have lost his savour" (Matt. 5:13) it becomes worthless. I imagine few people are ever saved entirely unaided by the influence of the church.[1]

—B. V. Seals
1898—1963
Evangelist and District Superintendent

I Am with You Alway

A perplexed child of God said that she was fearful lest God should leave her. How false is such a notion. And yet how many there are who live in such fear.

Does it seem possible that the Shepherd who sought the one lost sheep until He found it would leave it after He had gone through all the grief and suffering to redeem it? No! No! My fellow Christian. Jesus is seeking every opportunity to bless us, to reveal himself to us, to get deeper into our hearts and lives.

He promised, "Lo, I am with you alway, even unto the end of the world" (Matt. 28:20). He does not change with conditions. He is not dependent upon the state of your emotions. He is as near when the clouds are hovering over us, when we are in times of depression or in "heaviness through manifold temptation" (1 Pet. 1:6), as He is when the sun is shining brightly and when physically or mentally we may be in perfect condition.

Leave us? Why, He has sent the Holy Spirit into the world to abide with us forever. *Forever* surely does not suggest an occasional visit, or that He would trifle with us by playing hide-and-seek.

The chief purpose of this abiding Spirit is to make Jesus real to us. The person who lives in the fear of Jesus leaving him has not known what it is to experience that perfect love of Christ that casts out fear (see 1 John 4:18); a love that relies upon Him and His presence; a love that gives itself to Him in fellowship and communion; a love that trusts and has confidence in the Word of God. The great apostle said that nothing can separate us from the love of God (see Rom. 8:35).[2]

—D. Shelby Corlett
1867—1954
Editor

Abiding Produces Guidance

Jesus told the brokenhearted disciples as He was leaving them, "When the [Holy Ghost] is come, he will guide you into all truth" (John 16:13).

But away back before that the psalmist had said that "I will guide [you] with mine eye" (Ps. 32:8). When a man is guided with the eye of the Lord, he will get to the place that God intended him to just exactly on time, and he will fit into the place when he gets there, just like the stripes fit in the rainbow.

God looked in the direction that He wanted me to go; then He looked at me, and I hit the trail a-running, and thank the Lord, for these 40 years, by being led by His Spirit, upheld by His hand, protected by a wall of fire, and guided by His eye, I have been able to keep off of the breakers.

Many have been the plans that the devil has laid to defeat and wreck me, but just as often as the devil laid a plan to defeat me, God laid a plan to protect me; and when the devil stepped up and laid down a temptation before me, Jesus walked up and laid down a way of escape by the side of it, and the Holy Spirit whispered in my soul, "This is the way, walk ye in it" (Isa. 30:21). And by listening to His voice and obeying His commands, thank God, I stand before Him today with His wings over my head, with His everlasting arms beneath me, and with His love in my soul.

It is beautiful; it is glorious; it is beyond description. It looks like it is too good to be true, but thank God, it is so.[3]

—Bud Robinson
1860—1942
Evangelist

Keep Close to the Guide

"See then that ye walk circumspectly [carefully], not as fools, but as wise, redeeming the time, because the days are evil" (Eph. 5:15-16).

Watch your step. Walk strictly and accurately. Look around you before you put your foot down, remembering that rocks and sagebrush are full of rattlesnakes. The Greek word here for "circumspectly" suggests the walk of an acrobat. One misstep may mean disaster. How carefully we as Christians should walk in all diligence.

Watch your road. It is not always without stumbling stones. Moreover whether you travel the right road or the wrong, your way is an eternal one; it stretches away to infinity. If you keep on going in the present direction, what will be your destination at nightfall?

Watch your Guide. Though the pathway may at times lead over sharp rocks, up steep ascents, across streams filled with boulders, or traversing the hot desert sands, yet if you will observe carefully, you will find thereon the footprints of the Pierced Feet.

Walk wisely. Apply heart and brain to your behavior. Adopt a course of prudence. Be wise in your manner of dress, speech, and attitude; in your relationships with others; and in your use of material things.

Walk timely. Buy up your opportunities in the midst of these evil days. Wring out of the passing moments their highest possibilities.[4]

—Ross E. Price
1907-
Educator and Pastor

The Beauty of Jesus Captures Our Affections

The pleasures of sin will not be able to recapture our attention if we keep before us the beauty of Jesus and the joys of righteousness. Our hearts must respond to the glad affirmation of the psalmist: "Thou wilt shew me the path of life: in thy presence is fulness of joy; at thy right hand there are pleasures for evermore" (Ps. 16:11). Only in perfect love is there safety. The intensity of our devotion to Christ will be the measure of our strength to resist temptation and to withstand trial.[5]

—Richard S. Taylor
1912-
Theologian and Seminary Professor

The Workday Christ

He is not only the Christ for Sabbath morning—best clothes, pealing organ, open songbook, thrilling sermon, trained choirs—He is the Christ who comes in everyday dress, for everyday workshops and everyday toils: when we are controlling our business, tilling our fields, striking our anvils, pruning our trees, mending our children's clothes, cooking in the kitchen . . . He is a working-day Christ, in working-day clothes, for working-day hardships of working-day people.[6]

—J. B. Chapman
1884—1947
Editor and General Superintendent

The Satisfying Contentment of the Holy Life

A poor widow who never had quite enough of anything in her life stood for the first time on the shore of the ocean. With a great sigh of contentment she exclaimed, "Thank the Lord! There is something there's enough of."

Of the riches of God's grace there is enough and to spare. In the fields of God's plenty where His "grace is sufficient" (2 Cor. 12:9) for us, where "no good thing will he withhold from them that walk uprightly" (Ps. 84:11), where He "giveth us richly all things to enjoy" (1 Tim. 6:17), there we shall not want any good thing.

He has plenty to satisfy the deep cravings of our hearts so that we do not desire the chaff of the world, plenty so that we may live clean and strong in a world of sin, plenty so that we may share with others. Oh, the satisfied contentment of living in Canaan with its milk and honey.

All these are but a few of the natural resources of God's kingdom. Of ourselves we have no right to them, but trusting in the merits of the Man of Calvary we become heirs of God and joint heirs with Jesus Christ, and like Joshua we can have as much as we will press our feet of faith upon.

These riches of His grace are ours, not to exploit, but to use for the good of mankind and the glory of God.[7]

—John E. Riley
1909-
Pastor and College President

Keep Connected

Our relationship to God is like that of the motor to the dynamo. We must stay connected if we would keep supplied. The stored manna bred worms and became useless. Every morning the fresh supply must be gathered, and thus every morning contact with God must be established.

There is no single act of faith that answers for all time. "The just shall live by faith" (Rom. 1:17). There is no depositum of grace between the soul and the primary source—"But my God shall supply all your need according to his riches in glory by Christ Jesus" (Phil. 4:19).

If we could get spiritual supplies for an extended period, perhaps we, like the king's son, would forget to come to our Heavenly Father for that companionship that is of greater consequence than any detached "blessing" that could possibly come to us. But our continual dependence will not let us forget. "I need Thee every hour."[8]

—J. B. Chapman
1884—1947
Editor and General Superintendent

Staying Close to God on Ordinary Days

Walking symbolizes the humdrum of life, just the everyday, monotonous round of common things. For the housewife—the same dishes, the same beds, the same floors, the same laundry, the same plaguing need to suit the family's fastidious tastes. For the farmer—the same fields, the same animals, the same endless rotation of crops, the same struggle against frost and drought. With the businessman—the same office, the same endless chain of letters, the same hours of coming and going, the same relentless struggle to keep one's head above the swirl of modern business. With the man in the shop—the same time clock, the same roar and din, the same unchanging paycheck, the same meaningless grind. It is the humdrum of life that, after all, demands real heroism.

In many respects we do not need the grace of God so much to stand up against the crises—human pride and nature will aid us then. But we do need the grace of God to face 24 humdrum hours a day unflinchingly. The challenge of the saint is not particularly the martyr's death. It is the ability to go through the drudgery of each succeeding day in a Christian way.

The secret of all this is found in waiting on the Lord. That place of prayer is the storehouse of spiritual reserve. Prayer will help us not only to face the humdrum but also to face it gloriously.[9]

—H. V. Miller
1894—1948
General Superintendent

Victories Come in Small Packages

The right use of small things prepares a person for the power needed in the crises of life. Life is made up largely of small things. Many tragedies occur because of so-called trifles. It is also true that many of man's joys and good moments come through small things. A kind word in passing, a smile in a dark hour, a hearty handshake just at the right time have given the encouragement needed.

The secret of spiritual victory is in careful observance of the seemingly small things, being watchful of what may be termed "the stewardship of trifles." Jesus emphasized this when He mentioned giving a cup of water. It is a small matter to read a chapter of Scripture before starting the day, but it has saved many a person in the hour of temptation.

It may seem of little importance to breathe a prayer, but it may be like Elijah's prayer of 63 words on Mount Carmel, which brought the fire down. It may seem to be of small value to many, but the small example of a person going regularly to the house of God has been used by the Spirit to rebuke a wayward soul.

It may be only a few dollars for the cause of missions, but the spirit prompting it may loosen the purse strings of someone with abundant means. It seems as if many of God's blessings are bound up in the little things of life. May we always be faithful stewards in the little things.[10]

—Lewis T. Corlett
1896–1992
Educator

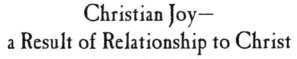

The Master Architect's Plan for Your Life

God, the Father, laid the plans from the foundation of time. No cost was spared. Heaven-sent came Jesus, the Only Begotten of the Father, to lay out the blueprint for life and to evidence the divine plan for a society built upon redeemed souls.

But we are sure we know more about how it should go than the eternal Architect, so each of us goes his own way. Observers look at the mess that has been created and scoff, "There wasn't an Architect in that situation. God is dead! Anyone could do better than that in planning a world."

Read again the intention of the Architect. "According as he hath chosen us in him before the foundation of the world, that we should be holy and without blame before him in love" (Eph. 1:4). There it is! That is the divine plan.[11]

—W. Shelburne Brown
1918-78
District Superintendent and College President

Christian Joy— a Result of Relationship to Christ

In the beginning of our Christian religion, one of the dominant notes was joy. We see the first Christians immediately following the outpouring of the Spirit on the Day of Pentecost breaking bread from house to house with gladness. From the time that the word had gone forth that Christ had risen from the dead, joy had sprung up in the hearts of Christ's followers, and amid the persecutions that beset their pathway still there was the note of rejoicing in God.

While there have been some religious movements of deep piety that have not had this characteristic note, yet it has been most evident in others. The Quakers seemed to find their emotional expression in contemplation and worship rather than in outbursts of joy, but with the early Methodists joy was a dominant factor, and so has it been with our own movement. Thus we might benefit by studying how John Wesley related joy to the Christian life.

Although Wesley maintained that joy characterized faith in Christ, yet it was a joy in God and not at all related to things of time and sense. He speaks of his own experience before he had entered into a state of acceptance with God. Examining himself he found certain states and conditions that he regarded not in keeping with the Christian experience. Of himself he said, "But I still hanker after creature happiness. My soul is almost continually running out after one creature or another and imagining how happy should I be in such or such a condition. I have more pleasure in eating and drinking and in the company of those I love than I have in God. I have relish for earthly happiness. I have not a relish for heavenly."

While Wesley found delight in the good things of earth—in good reading, for scarcely none read more widely than he; in science, which he studied eagerly; in music, and he attended a rendition of Handel's *Messiah*—yet he made none of these things the source of joy in his heart and life. He rejoiced in God. He often evaluated these things in their relationship to the Kingdom, but the fountain of life with its joyous dynamic rested alone in the redemption that Christ had wrought for him.[12]

—Olive M. Winchester
1880—1947
Theologian

The Glories of Old Age for Those Who Live Close to God

I like Dr. Chapman's encouragement for getting older.

He says they tell us our eyes are growing dim. No, they are not. God is merely darkening our sight to the things of this world that it may become better accustomed to the brighter world above. Our eyes must be perfected here, for there we shall behold the King in His beauty and the land of long distances.

They say that our hearing is failing, that we are growing deaf. No, we are not. God is merely stopping our ears to the noises of this world that they may be better tuned to the music of heaven. Then, too, our voices must be always clear, for not only shall we listen to seraphic choirs with harps of gold—perhaps a thousand strings—but we are also ourselves to join in the grand chorus of the skies: "Unto him that hath loved us, and washed us from our sins in his own blood . . . to him be glory and dominion for ever and ever" (Rev. 1:5).

They say that we are stooped with the burdens and cares of life that have pressed down so heavily upon us. No, we are not. We are simply practicing for the time when we shall bend low in reverence before the King of Kings and Lord of Lords and, casting our crowns before Him, shall crown Him Lord of all.[13]

—H. Orton Wiley
1877—1961
Theologian and College President

Christ Inspires Hope

The born-again Christian alone with a committed life has hope in these days of darkness. His hope is in Christ. Hope for a better day and security until that day comes are found in Christ alone.

Light for every night and courage for every fight, comfort for every sorrow and assurance for each tomorrow are found in Christ. He is the Pilot in every storm, the Victor over evil in every form. He alone is our Hope. A calm rest comes to my heart when I remember that "he is able to keep that which I have committed unto him against that day" (2 Tim. 1:12).

You may ask, "What day?" I declare, "This day—the day of disappointment, the day of sickness, the day of heartbreak, the day of death—just any day, you name it, and He is able to keep through it." Our hope is in Christ.[14]

—D. I. Vanderpool
1891—1988
General Superintendent

The Holy Spirit Guides the Believer

I was making the rounds of the museums in Florence, Italy. Applying the few rules of judging art that I knew, I moved quickly from one masterpiece to another. Then I noticed a group gathered around a picture that I had just left. The center of attention was the guide of the party, so I decided to listen in. He described the circumstances in the life of the artist that inspired him to select the subject of this work, and then explained the techniques the artist used to accent his motif. I was amazed to hear so many things that had completely escaped me. I needed the guidance service of an expert to understand what I was viewing.

One of the functions of the Holy Spirit is to guide us into all truth—the truth of what the promises of the Lord cover; the truth of the plan of salvation; the truth of the way the grace of God works in the lives of people; the truth that can be mined from the treasury of God's Word; the truth that can be gleaned from the various experiences of life; the truth that adds stature and maturity to our character; the truth that gives insight and meaning to life; the truth that opens new dimensions and fresh horizons to our vision; the truth that interprets the meaning and purpose of the secrets of everyday living.[15]

—Mendell Taylor
1912—2000
Seminary Professor

Using Trials

"In the world ye shall have tribulation: but . . ." (John 16:33).

Expect trials, fierce ones. They are normal for the Christian, normal and essential. Only fake remedies and scamped workmanship are put on the market without testing. Quack medicines and jerry-built houses do not invite the strain of trial; but God will not turn out a product that has not been tried and proved genuine.

Far from expecting trials, most of us expect—or hope—to get by without trial or persecution. When hard things come, we consider ourselves abused, treated unfairly, God-forgotten. We seek sympathy and pity ourselves. We forget there is nothing divine or Christian in an easy, unruffled life, no opportunity there to exhibit divine grace. It is the light shining in darkness that is seen.

Trials make us sharers with Christ; He suffered.

Tired? Remember His weary, footsore journeys. Unappreciated? Remember Him driven out of His own hometown. Misunderstood? Think of Him before Pilate. Lonely? Remember Gethsemane and the sleeping disciples. Ridiculed? Think of the purple robe and the crown of thorns. As you share with Him, He shares with you. He understands.

Rejoice in trial incurred because you are like Christ. For through it you can glorify Him. To glorify Christ is to show Christ's nature plain in you; it is to be identified with Deity. There can be no greater honor.[16]

—Bertha Munro
1887—1983
Educator

Comfortable in the Presence of God

A gentleman once said to his pastor, "How little salvation can I have and yet get into heaven. Do not answer me in terms of Scripture, nor with quotations from theology, but plainly as one man talking to another." In a word, he wanted to know what was the minimum of requirement to enter the holy city. Many others have desired the same information but have not dared to be as frank. The pastor answered, "You must have at least this much—enough to make you comfortable with God when you meet Him. Meet Him everyone must. Can one be comfortable with Him if the heart is full of sin, dark with hate, discolored with bitterness, rank with antagonism, and seared with iniquity?"

To ask is to answer such a question. And whatever a person with a sinful heart must have in order to qualify him for companionship in heaven with a holy God is the sum total of salvation and holiness of heart.[17]

—J. G. Morrison
1871—1939
General Secretary of World Missions

My Ship Is Soon to Sail

The apostle Paul was sending his final word to his young friend at Ephesus. The metaphor seemed fitting, so he added this cheering word, "The time is near, I am about to lift anchor and sail to the haven in the homeland on the other side of the sea" (2 Tim. 4:6). Loved ones and friends, he was sure, were awaiting his arrival—the prospect was alluring, and he was all but impatient to be away. As in the old sailing days, he watched every preparation with interest and solemn joy. Not that the journey itself mattered so much—it was the land beyond that enticed him.

But I, too, have sailed the seas. I, too, have felt the thrill of the hour for departing. I have felt the pull of the homeland beyond, and blessed the prospect of greeting loved ones and friends once more. And today I observe the intimations of an early departure for the final haven of my soul. The sails are filling; the shore-lines are being severed. The Skipper awaits the rising breeze. My ship is soon to sail. The ship is stout. May the passage be smooth! My loved ones await my landing. I am happy in the prospect. Let us lift the anchor and sail to the other side.[18]

—J. B. Chapman
1884—1947
Editor and General Superintendent

Easter Is the Drawbridge

Coming into Portland, Oregon, from Seattle, the train cross-es two rivers, the Columbia and the Willamette. Both rivers are navigable, and drawbridges carry the tracks. A little girl who had never seen a drawbridge was on one of these trains. As they ap-proached the first crossing, the bridge was open and the ap-proach was around a curve so that she could see where the rails ended and the wide expanse of water toward which the train was moving. She was terrified and clung to her mother in despera-tion. She said, "Mother! We're going right into the water." Her mother pointed to the bridge tender in the cage above the bridge. She said, "See the man up there? He will make a way across." As they watched, the gate tender pulled a lever and the bridge was closed so they could go across safely.

They soon came to the Willamette River crossing, and again the drawbridge was open. However, this time the little girl looked up until she saw the bridge tender. He was watching a tug pulling a log boom. It was almost through. Then he threw the lever and closed the bridge, and again the train moved across safely.

The little girl said, "Mother, I'm not afraid. There is always a man up there who makes a way across." When our soul comes to the river of death, there is a Man up there who has made a way across. Easter is the drawbridge.[19]

—Fletcher Galloway
1899—1988
Pastor

Friendship with Jesus

Jesus said, "Ye are my friends, if ye do whatsoever I command you" (John 15:14). This declaration takes us to the very heart of consecration. Too frequently consecration is regarded as a matter of giving up or giving away our rights to our own will. But in the truest sense Christian consecration is that attitude of heart that lays the foundation for fellowship with Christ. Thus, when we say "Thy will be done," we are not giving up or forfeiting something of great value; we are investing in the richest of experiences—friendship with Jesus.

The psalmist knew the blessedness of this truth when he said, "I will delight myself in thy commandments" (Ps. 119:47). The background for this declaration is found in other verses of that sixth division of the longest psalm: "I trust in thy word" (v. 42); "I have hoped in thy judgments" (v. 43); "I seek thy precepts" (v. 45); "I will meditate in thy statutes" (v. 48).

Thank God, there is an experience of joyous conformity to the whole will of God. There is provision through the atoning blood of Jesus for the cleansing of the heart from all that questions or rebels against the will of God. The pure heart finds glorious freedom in doing the full will of God, for in that will are found the highest possibilities for any personality, both subjectively and objectively.

So the true and final test of Christian discipleship is found, not in our creed or even our code of outward conduct, but rather in that deep and abiding spirit of glad obedience to Christ that establishes and maintains His "good, and acceptable, and perfect, will" (Rom. 12:2) as the supreme interest and end of our lives.

Friendship with Jesus!
Fellowship divine!
O what blessed, sweet communion!
Jesus is a Friend of mine. (STTL, 604)[20]

—Hugh C. Benner
1899—1975
General Superintendent

Deeper than the Stain Has Gone

All unworthy we who've wandered,
And our eyes are wet with tears
When we think of love that sought us
Through the dreary wasted years.
Yet we walk this holy highway,
For the pure in heart alone
Knowing Calvary's fountain reaches
Deeper than the stain has gone.

When with holy throng we're standing
In the presence of the King,
And our souls are lost in wonder
While the white-robed choirs sing,
Then we'll praise the name of Jesus
With the millions 'round the throne.
Praise Him for the love that reaches
Deeper than the stain has gone.[21]

—Raymond Browning
1879—1953
Evangelist and Poet

When Jesus Comes

When our Lord returns, one look at that matchless face will forever banish the need of hospitals, medicines, doctors, and nurses. Coffins and cemeteries will have become obsolete. In that face is an antidote for every ill, a balm for every pain, and a cure for every infirmity. No groan or cough or sigh will ever fall again upon the listening ear. No germ will ever again infest the air. At His coming, the sick shall be cured, the lame made whole, the dead raised to life, and "this corruptible must put on incorruption, and this mortal must put on immortality" (1 Cor. 15:53).[22]

—Jarrette Aycock
1890—1966
District Superintendent

Singing—a Strategy for Abiding

Imagine a world without music. No trumpets to announce the great. No orchestrations to celebrate a victory. No bands for marching troops. No choirs on the Sabbath, no congregational singing. Not even a hymn when the dead is put away. Empty world.

God is a musician. He makes the "melody of the spheres." His creation serenades Him. Ten million feathered choristers fill the world with song. The wind has a bugle; and the brooks sing on their way to the sea. I have heard the pines humming an evening song. I have heard an elephant trumpet, and I thought he was saluting his Creator.

How much music there is in the Old Testament! Cornets, cymbals, dulcimers, flutes, harps, timbrels, organs, pipes, psalteries, sackbuts, taborets, trumpets, and viols. They sounded in the Tabernacle and in the Temple. They thundered with the marching men of Israel.

The songs of David drift down the centuries and lift us on symphonic tides. Over and over again the psalmist exhorts his people to sing. "Sing aloud." he cries. He knew the power of music to lift the soul.

The end of the Bible is a song—a white-robed throng singing of earth's redemption by the blood of the Lamb. "I heard the voice of harpers harping with their harps: and they sung as it were a new song before the throne" (Rev. 14:2-3).

Of course. There is no heaven without music. The God who wrought the nature we have known, who put in man such universal love of melody, and the overwhelming urge to make it, would not build a heaven without an orchestra and a choir. There will be music there! Beethoven and Bach will dwindle to bird-whistles before the towering tones of the celestial song service. Even *I* shall sing then. These inharmonious vocal chords shall break forth, joined in a cantata that shall roll from the golden streets to the lifted domes of New Jerusalem! And maybe Bud Robinson and I will sing a duet.[23]

—Lon R. Woodrum
1901-95
Evangelist

4 ❋ "Feed on His Word"
The Bible—A Guidebook for Holy Living

From the time of the Early Church the Bible has enabled serious Christians to see God in Jesus and to see God at work in molding biblical characters into holy people. This old Book of God keeps speaking with authenticity and authority to each new generation. In some unfathomable way the Bible's eternal message is always contemporary, and its timeless truths are as up to date as this morning's TV newscast. One new believer called it God's love letter to His family.

Whether one is a first-time reader or a veteran Scripture reader, the Bible speaks to life and calls us to the values of the heavenly world. And those who think the Bible a boring, hard-to-understand book are delighted to find that when the Holy Spirit comes in fullness, Scripture becomes more understandable, more interesting, and even more fascinating.

Critics have questioned or even attacked the Bible, but long after they are dead and gone, the Book of God continues to impact civilization and to enrich individuals. From the beginning, the Nazarenes have believed the Bible to be God's Word that contains everything necessary to faith and the practice of a life of holiness.

Even better than the stately old trees in the most mature forest, the Bible has lived through droughts, fires, infestations, and neglect. It lives and it speaks. I love Abraham Lincoln's advice, "Take all this book upon reason that you can, and the balance on faith, and you will live and die a happier and better person."[1]

—Neil B. Wiseman

The Magnetic Christ of the Bible

Jesus Christ is the Answer to every need in the imagery of the blessed Bible. To the hungry He is Bread. To the thirsty He is Water. To the sick He is Physician and Healing Balm. To the accused He is Advocate at court. To the condemned He brings pardon. He opens the prison to those already incarcerated. To those whose lives are wasted He gives beauty for ashes. He is the Rose of Sharon for beauty, the Lily of the Valley for purity, the Morning Star for hope, the Lamb of God for atonement, and "a great rock in a weary land" and "a Shelter in the time of storm" (see STTL, 424, 571).

He is the Lion of the tribe of Judah for power, and in this function He breaks every chain and gives us the victory again and again. He is Money to the poor, Wisdom to the ignorant, and Holiness to the defiled. And if there be a prayer for which no fitting word can be found, then He is the Answer to that, too, for He is "the desire of all nations" (Hag. 2:7).

When Jesus was here in the flesh, He never met His match, although He was challenged at every step. Denied a place in the palace, He was born a King in a stable. Refused the adoration of sages, He was worshiped by shepherds. Since no Levites came to chant, angels sang His Christmas carol. The great did not apply for tuition in His school, so He chose humble fishermen and despised tax gatherers to be His disciples.

Being himself a Miracle, the normal atmosphere of His life was friendly to miracles. People regularly came to ask Him to do the impossible. And after admitting it to be impossible, they went right along and asked Him to do it.

When taxes came due and the purse was empty, the first fish taken at the Master's command furnished money for double taxes. When 10,000 people came to Him in the desert, He fed them all without opening a fish market or founding a bakery. Ten lepers were healed by the word of His power all in a group. Maimed, halt, blind, leprous, palsied—all were alike to Him. He healed them all. When the boat went away and left Him, He made a pavement of the sea and reached His destination on time. When the restless waves would flood the ship on which He rode, He calmed them as a mother would put her feverish child to sleep. He broke up the only funeral He ever attended by restoring the dead youth alive to his mother. "It is fortunate," says D. L. Moody, "that He called the name of Lazarus that day when He said, 'Come forth.' For otherwise all the dead would have come at His invitation, as they will yet do sometime."

His whole life was vicarious and substitutionary. He came down to our world that we might go up to His world. He was born in a stable and cradled in a manger that He might get down beneath us all and lift us up to God. He was "despised and rejected of men" (Isa. 53:3) that we might be accepted of God and admired by angels forevermore. He walked the dirt roads of our world that we might walk the golden streets of heaven. He bore a cross that we might wear a crown. He drank vinegar mingled with gall that we might drink the water of life. He wore a crown of thorns that we might wear a crown of life. He was with the wicked in His death that we might be with the righteous in everlasting life. He was lifted up upon a Cross that we might be lifted up upon a throne. He went down into the grave that we might come up out of the grave in the glory of His resurrection. He took our place on earth that we might share His place in heaven forever.[2]

—**J. B. Chapman**
1884—1947
Editor and General Superintendent

The Influence of Scripture on Pioneer Nazarenes

Our forefathers read the Bible persistently, eagerly, prayerfully; and as they read its sacred pages, they heard holy men of God speak "as they were moved by the Holy Ghost" (1 Pet. 1:21). To them, "All scripture is given by inspiration of God, and is profitable for doctrine, for reproof, for correction, for instruction in righteousness: that the man of God may be perfect, throughly furnished unto all good works" (2 Tim. 3:16-17). To them the Bible was entirely trustworthy. Hence they gladly ordered their lives by its teachings and committed their souls for time and eternity to One who spoke to them in His Word and said, "Heaven and earth shall pass away, but my words shall not pass away" (Matt. 24:35). They were convinced they had found a safe guide in God's Word.

When they found their lives below the standard of God's Word, they tampered not with its plain teachings but rather sought the grace it promised. Thus, instead of seeking to bring the Scriptures down to the level of men's lives, they sought always to bring men's lives up to the level of the Scriptures. To them the final arbiter in all matters of faith and practice was, "What saith the Lord?"[3]

—Hardy C. Powers
1900-1972
General Superintendent

The Bible Communicates a Life of Victory

The Bible rings with the shouts of victory and triumph to those who obey the call of God; but it is filled with the groans and sad wails of the fainthearted and disobedient, from Eden's beautiful garden to the final end of the pending tribulation.

The life of Joshua was one succession of victories, from that day until the day of his death, when he called the elders and all Israel to record to hear his dying testimony: "Ye know in all your hearts and in all your souls, that not one thing hath failed of all the good things which the LORD your God spake concerning you; all are come to pass unto you, and not one thing hath failed thereof" (Josh. 23:14). What a testimony, but hear the admonition: "If ye do in any wise go back, . . . know for a certainty that the Lord your God will no more drive out any of these nations from before you" (vv. 12-13).

If God ever needed a Joshua, He needs a man today who will stem the tide of worldliness and formality that has crept into the church of today, and rout the demon of lifelessness in this pleasure-crazed and money-mad age. Will you furnish the man?[4]

—C. B. Jernigan
1863—1930
District Superintendent

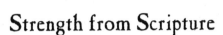

Strength from Scripture

Just as sunlight when conducted through a prism is broken down into its various rays, so the light of God's truth when filtered through the prisms of human personalities of the Scripture writers who took on the varying slants and interests of those personalities. That is shown not only in the language used—both vocabulary and style—but also in actual thought-forms, in ways of approach, in diversity of emphasis. The Holy Spirit used the varying interests and emphases of the different writers to convey the total of divine revelation in the Bible.[5]

—Ralph Earle
1907-95
Seminary Professor

A Prayer for Making Scripture Vital

Thy Word is a Lamp; make it a Light to us today. Give me a sure word, untainted by speculation or closet-room philosophy, for these men and women are troubled and vexed by suffering and sin. Help me make Thy Word plain today so that children will understand and old folks will not go away disappointed. Help me to challenge strong men and women with a word that is timeless and eternal.

Give me an assuring word. Some will be there who have lost

their way. Give me that redemptive word that will bring them back, penitent.[6]

—Samuel Young
1901-90
General Superintendent

Test Your Conduct by Scripture

Any leading or impression that may come should have a rigid comparison with the Word of God. The Spirit of God never leads anyone contrary to the written Word of God. The Spirit and the Word agree. When there is the least divergence from the spirit of the Word, or conflict with any passage of the letter of the Word of God, the leading or impression is from the devil.[7]

—C. W. Ruth
1865—1941
Associate Pastor to Bresee

God Leads His
Dear Children Through Scripture

If people walk with God, they must walk where He walks. "He leadeth me in the paths of righteousness for his name's sake" (Ps. 23:3). This old path of righteousness is the very one that Abel walked at the beginning of human history, when he had witness borne to him that he was righteous.

This is the only path that God ever did or ever will walk in. From eternity He has ever been the same holy Being. Man's fashions and customs change. He smiles on this today and on that to-morrow; but "[God is] the same yesterday, and to-day, and for ever" (Heb. 13:8). Men run daft after every new thing, new theology, new criticism, new philosophies, new religion, new beliefs.

Even John Wesley's "perfect love" is relegated to the back shelf or the lumber room. No religious notion over 20 years old is counted worthy of respect. But God looks down calmly upon all this fickle foolishness and says, "Ask for the old paths, where is the good way, and walk therein" (Jer. 6:16).

It requires no ordinary courage to do it in these days, when men bow, as willows in a gale, before any fashionable craze of unbelief; and backboneless preachers and people alike would rather be popular than be right with God. God's path is the path of holiness. "And an highway shall be there, and a way, and it shall be called The way of holiness; the unclean shall not pass over it, for he shall be with them" (Isa. 35:8, marginal reading).

This is why God asks people to get their hearts cleansed. Without that cleansing they never will peaceably walk His road.[8]

—A. M. Hills
1848—1951
Theologian and College President

What the Bible Teaches About Sin

Sin is the most expensive thing in the world. It cost God the perfect, eternal peace that had always been His. Sin cost the world its first and only Eden and turned it into a place of chaos, floods, thorns, storms, and earthquakes. It wrote the pages of history in blood. Sin has scarred the face of the globe with ugly graves. Sin built every hospital and every prison. Sin is to blame for every broken home, every broken body, every broken heart, every broken life.

Sin has made man a beast of burden, loaded down by guilt. Sin has erected barriers, broken fellowship, and split churches, families, and friends. Sin has caused men to hate, to fight, to lower themselves to the level of the animal. Sin has brought guilt, remorse, and despair, taking away sunshine, peace, and hope. Sin has blighted character and destroyed self-respect.

Is it any wonder that God hates sin as He does? Yet He has

given His Son to die in our place to provide forgiveness and reconciliation. Live above sin through the power of His Holy Spirit. That power is available to you today.[9]

—Fletcher Spruce
1913-74
Pastor and District Superintendent

5 ❊ "Make Friends of God's Children"

Relationships—the Church's Reason for Being

◦—◦ ⟪◦⟫ ◦—◦

Happy, holy relationships make churches authentic and attractive. Rich, meaning-packed words such as "fellowship," "friendship," "service," "community," "love," and "care" describe and define the community of faith. And because Nazarenes believe holiness of heart and life cannot be lived in isolation, they build congregations that seem a lot like extended human families where everybody feels a sense of belonging. Sometimes they even call each other brother and sister.

To be a Nazarene is to be part of a global family that seeks to be radically Christian—a loving, healing, authoritative, and compelling influence on the world.

This section of the book has several references showing how the Church of the Nazarene sees itself as a part of the historic Body of Christ. Friendship, service, and fellowship were key ingredients in the lives of all who made up the Church of the Nazarene in the early days, and that value continues until today.

—Neil B. Wiseman

A Prayer for the Church

God and Father of our Lord Jesus Christ, look upon us here today and deliver us from the curse that comes upon religious bargain hunters. Help us to count the cost of things that are indispensable, and then help us to pay that price, as our fathers used to do. Thou hast not changed, and our needs are ever the same. In our bargaining we have obtained but inferior goods. We ask for the heartache and the heartbreak and the tears and the signs that in all the days of the past have presaged the sort of spiritual awakening that we now crave. Deliver us from smugness and unfounded content. Give us that deep love for thyself and Thy Church that has always acted as an expulsive power to force out all opposites. And give us the souls of men for whom Christ died. Amen, and amen.[1]

—J. B. Chapman
1884—1947
Editor and General Superintendent

The Church—a Place Where All Are Welcomed at the Throne

God's love is not limited to the crowned heads, to the great and mighty; He loves the poor, the ignorant, the vile; He brings hope to the hopeless, help to the helpless, love to the unlovely, peace to the miserable, and salvation to the lost. The harlot at the well of Samaria, the woman with seven devils are precious in His sight. To these He speaks peace in their souls—causes wells of water to spring up into life everlasting. The prodigal is never allowed to stand cold and hungry at His gate. All are welcomed to inherit the riches and the comforts of His kingdom. "Whosoever will, let him [come and] take the water of life freely" (Rev. 22:17) is God's universal invitation to the souls of men.[2]

—R. T. Williams Sr.
1883—1946
General Superintendent

The Church as a Place of Service Was God's Idea

The church is under divine orders and protection and can never fail so long as she fulfills her commission and does His will. Why this emphasis? The answer is obvious. It is right and the one way and only way to succeed. All departments of the church must have a common goal, a common purpose, a central theme, a common passion. What is that one passion, that one coordinating purpose? God. He is the Answer.

Here is the final word concerning the business of the church, namely, to do His will. What is His will for us all and for the church? It is to cooperate with Him in His purposes and plans to save the world. His objective must be ours. His purposes must be ours. His passion must be ours. What is that plan? To save men. Thus, God has blessed the church because she has loved God and labored for souls. Let this not be forgotten in the tomorrows.

A casual glance at church history will reveal the reasons for the success of some churches and the failure of others. The successful church emphasized the basic essentials. The defeated church gave its time and attention too much to things merely incidental. Ability to distinguish between the important and the less important marks the line between assentation and dissension.

Occasionally an individual with good intention, but with misguided judgment, tries to lead the church to a wrong emphasis, but always the church refuses to be thus led astray, or onto sidetracks. We are determined to stick to our central theme. Secondary values are not to be despised, but properly evaluated and subordinated to the supreme values, where they can properly serve their purpose.[3]

**—General Superintendents' Quadrennial Address
to the 10th General Assembly**

Souls for Christ—Our Goal

Souls have been the goal of the church. These have been second only to love for Christ. The church has never been with us an end, but always a means to an end, namely, souls. To this end every department of the church must operate, together with all institutions. Church buildings, schools, departmental organizations, revivals, preaching, budgets, must all be directed to the salvation of souls. Let this conviction deepen, that our one business is to cooperate with God in saving souls.[4]

**—General Superintendents' Quadrennial Address
to the 10th General Assembly**

Go to the Front Lines

The front line is always right next to you. The man who works next to you, the woman who sits at the next desk, the one who is sitting by you on the bus, train, or plane, the family living in the next apartment or next door—these are the front line for you. Right here is where we so often fail. We have our eyes on the needs far away. But the harvest field is right next to each of us. If we Christians can only learn this, we will simplify our task. There is always someone near who needs our Savior. Jesus tried hard to get us to see it. He endeavored earnestly to make us realize that we need to get our Christian faith to work in the common things or everyday living. The Church has so often and so long waited for God to do the supernatural to awaken a generation. But Christ commanded us to pray, preach, witness, and work for souls. If we will do this, the great awakening we hope and pray for will come, and men will cry out, "The LORD he is God" (Ps. 100:3).[5]

**—V. H. Lewis
1912—2000
General Superintendent**

The Unified Church in Fellowship

The record of the Day of Pentecost reveals and emphasizes the fact that the Christian disciples in the Upper Room "were all with one accord in one place" (Acts 2:1). Later in the same chapter we read, "And they continued stedfastly in the apostles' doctrine and fellowship" (v. 42). Much has been made of the element of doctrinal agreement, but we need to realize that along with this there was a constant fellowship. Again we read how they continued "daily with one accord in the temple, and breaking bread from house to house" (v. 46). This beautiful Christian spirit prevailed in their later experience, for near the close of the fourth chapter of Acts we are told that "the multitude of them that believed were of one heart and of one soul" (v. 32).

The unity of the Holy Spirit pervaded the Church of Pentecost. Self-seeking, personal ambition, desire for preferment, jealousy, and all kindred carnal attitudes and dispositions had been cleansed from their hearts by the fiery baptism with the Spirit. The fruit of the Spirit was being evidenced in their lives—"love, joy, peace, longsuffering, gentleness, goodness, faith, meekness, temperance" (Gal. 5:22-23). Such fruitage always produces unity.

But unity does not necessitate uniformity. In that early group there was a vast variety of personalities. God always has recognized the value of individuality. But in the midst of their individual differences they had found, in the Spirit, a basis for a deep and abiding unity. By the help of God they were able to subordinate the lesser elements of personal opinion, differences in judgment, and variety of outlook to the major issues of Christian living and service.[6]

—Hugh C. Benner
1899—1975
General Superintendent

The Meaning of the Name "Nazarene"

When the organization that was later to be known as the Church of the Nazarene was first formed, various persons were requested to suggest names for the movement that was being so blessed of God.

Reacting from the worldliness and spiritual insincerity that he had found among the wealthier churches, Dr. Bresee was at that time laboring among the poor. In requesting a supernumerary relation from his conference, he had been given permission to organize a mission among the poor in the city of Los Angeles. Under the illumination of the Spirit he had seen "that the first service of the Holy Ghost baptized church is to the poor; that its ministry is to those who are lowest down; that its gifts are for those who need them most. As the Spirit was upon Jesus to preach the gospel to the poor, so His Spirit is upon His servants for the same purpose. As, when on earth, Jesus declared the crowning evidence of His divine mission to be that 'the poor have the gospel preached to them' [Matt. 11:5]; so today the evidence of the presence of Jesus in our midst is that we bear the gospel, primarily to the poor."

Various names were suggested for the organization at a meeting called for that purpose. Some of these names were connected with Methodism; some of them, entirely independent. It remained for Dr. Widney, then associated with Dr. Bresee in the work, a godly man and a brilliant lawyer, to suggest the name "Church of the Nazarene." He offered as reasons for his suggestion that the mission that had been divinely given to this organization was to the poor; and second, that it would necessarily be a mission of reproach because of its insistence upon entire sanctification with consequent opposition to worldliness.

To us there is no name more alluring, more challenging, or more significant than the name "Nazarene," which the Scriptures apply to our Lord. And this same quiet beauty and significance attaches to "Church of the Nazarene." There is something about the name that is so alluring and compelling that it draws us instinctively into sympathy with Jesus and His mission to the poor, the neglected, and the oppressed.

Preaching in the old wooden tabernacle, Dr. Bresee, speaking of the mission of the Church of the Nazarene, further said, "As Peter and John stood that day before the inquiring crowd, so we today stand before the vast work of saving men. We have nothing in or of ourselves. No human utterance is anything. No human power can do anything. We stand in our weakness and helplessness simply to tell men of the marvelous name. . . . We have to pry under a thousand souls and every one must lift! Lift every pound of strength. Lift till we see stars. Lift till we see beyond the stars. But, brethren, we may lift till every eye is strained from its socket, and it will do no good if Jesus of Nazareth walk not in the midst.[7]

—H. Orton Wiley
1877—1961
Theologian and College President

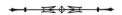

Peter—an Example of a Sanctified Personality Serving God

A Man plus God. Peter is Peter after as before Pentecost. He has lost none of his natural human instincts.

He still is talkative; but his chattering has changed to witnessing for Jesus.

His boasting has become holy boldness; when he says "we ought to obey God rather than men" (Acts 5:29), he has the inward strength to make good his defiance.

He still takes the lead, but the selfish braggadocio is gone; the impulsiveness is under control; his own interests are lost in Christ's.

And the Spirit has taught him the meaning of the Cross. Personality is not destroyed nor absorbed by the incoming of Deity; it is purged of its dross, unified, energized.

Peter still is a live wire and a leader, but he has learned that human energy and enthusiasm are not sufficient to carry him through. His dependence is on his contact with God. He must obey, and he must pray. He must keep himself in the love of God. Even the first Pentecost did not make sainthood automatic.[8]

—Bertha Munro
1887—1983
Educator

The Springtimes of Service

The Church of Jesus Christ should know periodic springtimes. Dry times will come. Winter may send the chilling frost. But the God of eternal spring will send the renewing showers of grace to the soul so that the grass turns green, the birds sing, the flowers bloom, and the trees and fields bear abundant harvest. However clearly we may have been born of the Spirit and baptized with the Spirit, we still need renewings of the Spirit.[9]

—John E. Riley
1909-
Pastor and College President

The Opportunity of a Century Is Ours Now

The Church of the Nazarene must be sane, but we must be aggressive. We must be considerate and liberal toward others, but we cannot wait because of conventionalities. We must conduct revivals and organize churches everywhere. We must establish revival centers in all the large cities in the land. We must establish and build up 50 camp meetings, at least one for each district in the church.

The idea that we should live on the defensive is a mistaken one. Preaching "against" the heresies of the age will not meet the need. We must preach a positive, delivering gospel. Offering a "home" for such Holiness people as are not offered asylum by others is but a small part of our mission. We must go out into the forest and fell our own timber and build of our own material. We are not shifting responsibility or seeking rest and passivity; we are to launch into a battle that will demand all our resources and make us targets for the devil and for religious mossbacks everywhere. The times are ripe. The Church of the Nazarene has the opportunity of a century. Shall we enter the rich fields and gather in the harvest that is awaiting the efforts of a sane, straight, aggressive Holiness church?[10]

—J. B. Chapman
1884—1947
Editor and General Superintendent

Authentic Worship
Increases Spiritual Strength

The 84th psalm is usually interpreted as the longing of the servant of God for the worship of the sanctuary: "My heart and my flesh crieth out for the living God" (v. 2). We do not read far into the psalm until we realize that this is not an expression of longing for the customary ritual, nor for the songs of the Tabernacle, nor for the prayers commonly used in the Temple. It is an expression of deep heart-longing for the conscious presence of God as living Helper, Guide, and Comforter.

The psalmist points out four functions of worship. Worship helps us to realize our nearness to God until we cry out, "How amiable [how lovely] are thy tabernacles, O LORD of hosts!" (v. 1).

Worship expresses the deepest longing of the heart and soul: "My heart and my flesh crieth out for the living God" (v. 2).

Worship gives a sense of being "at home" with God until one exclaims, "My King, and my God" (v. 3).

Worship intensifies the spirit of gratitude and praise:

"Blessed are they that dwell in thy house: they will be still praising thee" (v. 4).

What a comprehensive summary of the elements of worship: nearness to God, longing for God, a sense of "oneness" with God, and praise to God. Through such an experience of worship we become conscious of a strength derived from God. It creates springs of refreshment in the wilderness and constantly renews and increases spiritual strength. Little wonder we are urged to "consider one another to provoke unto love and to good works: not forsaking the assembling of ourselves together" (Heb. 10:24-25).[11]

—Mary L. Scott
1909-96
General Secretary of Nazarene World Mission Society

———— ✦ ————

Flood Tides of Revival Motivate Our Service

Springing wells and *flowing rivers* symbolize being born of the Spirit and being filled with the Spirit. But in the Scripture lesson you will note a third measure of water mentioned, "I will pour . . . *floods* upon the dry ground" (Isa. 44:3, italics added). The floods that God says He will pour upon the dry ground symbolize revivals, refreshings, and anointings that He is pleased to give to His Church and to individuals.

The need today among our people is not a new church, but a revival that will renew the old church; a revival that will cause people to clean out the old wells of former years, remove the trash and rubbish that the world has piled in, and let the living waters begin to spring again—a revival that will be like a mighty flood sweeping down a river. It is remarkable what a flood will do when turned loose. It will clean out old stagnated pools, straighten out crooks and bends in the river, cut new channels, and remove old snags and old drifts that may have hindered the river's flow for many months.

I saw an old hickory tree, not far from our home in Missouri, that a high wind had caused to fall across the creek. Its roots were fastened on one side of the creek and its branches stuck deep in the mud on the other side. It formed a perfect barrier across the creek. Everything that came down the creek lodged against the old hickory. It is amazing what will come down a creek in a period of months—logs, brush, leaves, cornstalks, dead animals, cats, squirrels. After months this old tree, with its attending drift, finally soured and the stench became a menace in the neighborhood. . . .

Then the flood came, sweeping everything in front of it. Railroad embankments went out; steel rails were wrapped around huge trees. Backwater from the flood covered the fields and floated barns and houses away. Large fish from the Missouri River came out across the fields, leaving in their wake rippling waves that appeared as if a small canoe had been along.

After about three weeks the flood went down and we went back to investigate the damage. We went to see what happened to the old hickory. We walked along the creek and searched carefully. We could not find the least sign of the old drift that was there. There was not a root or branch to mark the spot. The flood had swept it all away—the drift was gone.

As that cloudburst in southern Iowa released a flood that swept out the old hickory, just so God proposes to open the floodgates and give revivals that will sweep through the church—revivals that will change, transform, and renew until old hindrances, logs, snags, and drifts are swept away, leaving the church with an unobstructed channel through which the Holy Ghost can operate unhindered.[12]

—D. I. Vanderpool
1891—1988
General Superintendent

Authentic Worship of God Impacts Service

Worship is the true basis of successful church life. To attempt to develop a church organization that shall possess spirituality and stability without observing the principles that underlie all true worship is to hopelessly fail. We have often been pained at the lack of worship in many of our church services. Worship should exalt God. It should praise His perfections, commune with Him through the Spirit, offer to Him the heart's sincere adoration, draw freely upon the resources of divine grace, and in everything—by word and deed—exalt the Christ of God. What then of a service where human efforts are magnified, human attainments praised, and human strength alone exalted. A service where the songs deal almost wholly with subjective human attainments rather than divine grace, where the sermon is a literary or oratorical triumph, and where the prayers are in a very real sense addressed to the congregation—what can be said of such a service as judged by the standards of true worship? . . .

A service of true worship must make God real to the worshipers. Unless the Spirit of God is present, through whom fellowship and communion with the Father and Son are established, there can be no real worship. The songs, sermon, prayers and testimonies must be the media through which the truth of God bursts forth; but without the Spirit, all these things are dead and lifeless. The human heart needs God, and unless the service brings men to the depths of soul communion through the Spirit, men will not be loyal to it. Samuel Rutherford, the fragrance of whose piety remains rich to the present day, urged upon his people the necessity of a growing communion with their Lord. "There are curtains to be drawn aside in Christ," he says, "that we never saw, and new foldings of love in Him. I despair that I shall ever win to the far end of that love, there are so many plies in it. Therefore dig deep and sweat and labor and take pains for Him and set by as much time in the day for Him as you can. He will be won in the labor."[13]

—H. Orton Wiley
1877—1961
Theologian and College President

Opportunity for Service Never Better

The next five decades are ours for the taking. Of course there are troubles among us. There is bickering and fussing and displays in plenty of a failure to possess the wondrous experience for which we stand. But that is not altogether an evil sign. There are individual churches of other denominations by the thousand that have no troubles; they are as peaceful as a corpse and just as dead. Trouble, division, strife are as often as not a sign that we have life enough to warrant an attack of the enemy. Flowing water is usually a bit troubled and was designated by Jewish writers as *living water*. Perfectly peaceful water is too often stagnant. Where there is life there is agitation, and this sometimes manifests itself in differences of opinion. Water never turns a mill wheel without turbulence. All machinery develops friction unless most plentifully oiled. Friction, hotboxes, and smoking bearings are no call to abandon the machine, but are a loud summons for the big oilcan. Pour on the oil; don't stop the machine. Prayer, grace, tenderness, unselfishness, the mind of Christ, the unction, the anointing of the Holy Ghost—these are the lubricating oils for our Nazarene machine.

But forward; we have the message of the hour. Entire Christian holiness, the death route of full salvation, selfishness slain, the old man crucified, the burning afflatus of the Spirit eradicating carnality—these are what earnest groups of souls all over the world hunger for. Nazarenes are among their present-day custodians.

One hundred percent Christianity! The field is almost free from competition. The opposition is the same old sin, the same old world, and the same old devil, for all of which we have a wondrous cure. The Holiness churches can take the age if they will.[14]

—J. G. Morrison
1871—1939
General Secretary of World Missions

Worship Affects Everything Else

What is the supreme purpose of the church toward which every subsidiary organization must contribute and from which no organization must be allowed to draw? This is to be found in its worship. Worship is the rallying center, the unifying principle, the basic need, without which churches would have no existence.

By worship we mean, not a ritualistic service of prepared forms of expression, nor do we mean the gathering of a careless people without depth of earnestness or spiritual life, but the coming of a soul into the presence of God. Ritualism, however reverent and beautiful, easily tends to become formal, while un-ritualistic services easily degenerate into meetings for instruction or entertainment.

The public services of the Church of the Nazarene must mean the coming of the congregation into the presence of God through the Spirit. It must mean the tarrying on the portals of the upper sanctuary until the power of the Holy Ghost falls upon the waiting worshipers.

Under the illumination of the Holy One, the souls of the redeemed burst into holy song, and lips touched with living fire speak forth the matchless glories of Him who has redeemed them. Under this unction from the Holy One the soul of the preacher glows and burns like a seraph, and through his ministry, there bursts in upon the minds and hearts of his people a vision of God and divine things. It is in the light of this spiritual vision that sinners see their lost condition and make their way repentant to an altar of prayer.[15]

—H. Orton Wiley
1877—1961
Theologian and College President

6 ❋ "Help Those Who Are Weak"

Willing Love Slaves for God

Service is tricky for many Christians. Often a job needs doing, so we do it out of obligation or as a favor to somebody who recruited us. Serving for the right reasons may not have much to do with the impact of our service, but it has a lot to do with us and the kind of Christians we are becoming.

The weak in the song "Take Time to Be Holy" and the weak in our lives refers to everybody. Everyone we know is sometimes weak and needs us. And in our own weakness we often need others too.

Commonly, service is considered to be doing something for someone in God's name. But another dimension has to be considered. Serving is a precious gift God gives us so we can be used by a great cause. So when I preach, teach, or offer a cup of cold water in our Lord's name, I am connected to the greatest cause in the world.

Mother Teresa of Calcutta shines a bright light on motives and values for serving with this insight: "There is always the danger that we may just do the work for the sake of the work. This is where the respect and the love and the devotion come in—that we do it for God, for Christ, and that's why we try to do it as beautifully as possible."[1]

The Nazarene writers from yesteryear believed that the empowering energy of the Holy Spirit makes service the natural outcome of sanctification. And with that conviction they impacted their world for Christ.

—Neil B. Wiseman

Love Is Not Afraid to Give Too Much

The philosophy of the Good Samaritan was this: What's mine is ours and we will share it. This is in direct controversy with the philosophy that is abroad in the world and says, What's yours is mine and I am going to have it.

In the early days of the Bible Society in Russia, many sacrifices were necessary to keep the work going. The peasants who had been given the gospel light by this means were anxious to contribute their share for its continuation. The occasion for the offering came. As the people were passing by the collection plate and making their gifts, a very poor Russian woman cheerfully gave her lone ruble. Some friends noticing the incident later remarked to her that she had given too freely out of her meager earnings. In quick response to this suggestion, the Christian heroine replied, "Love is not afraid of giving too much."

Love is the basis for all true Christian service. How much shall I give? The answer is plain—to the extent of my ability and the limit of my love. "God so loved . . . that he gave his only begotten Son" (John 3:16). Christ gave His all that we might be free. We can do no less than offer ourselves in full consecration and willing obedience to the Lord of life. To love God supremely and our fellowmen sincerely—this is the motive supreme. This is the goal of the "life with a plus." To be spent for God is life's crowning glory.[2]

—Sylvester T. Ludwig
1903-64
General Secretary

Devotion, the Price of Service

Service is not a substitute for devotion; service expresses devotion in practical living. "If any man serve me, let him follow me"

(John 12:26). Here Jesus indicates that devotion is the true price of service. We cannot serve God our own way; it must be His way.[3]

—Samuel Young
1901-90
General Superintendent

All Out for Souls

Brethren, I was born in the fire, and I cannot endure the smoke. I am a child of the bright daylight, and mists and fogs and depressing gloom are not to my liking. I want to go all out for souls. The revival I seek is not the product of the labors of some personality-plus evangelist. Such a revival is too detached and impersonal to meet my needs or to answer my prayers. I want that kind of revival that comes in spite of the singing, the preaching, the testimonies, and the human attractions and detractions. I want that kind of revival because it takes that kind to really revive me.

I want a revival that, like a summer shower, will purify the atmosphere of our churches everywhere and that will awaken the dormant forces of our people young and old. I want something so general and so divine that it will be uncontrollable. I want something that will reemphasize old-time moral and spiritual conditions. Something that will reform and regenerate drunkards and save respectable worldlings. Something that will bring in the youth and the little children. Something so attractive that it will break over into the circles of the pleasure loving. Something that will set people on their back tracks to make restitution for wrongs committed. Something that will bring God to bear upon our domestic problems to save our people from the twin evils of divorce and race suicide. Something that will inject old-time honesty, veracity, purity, and otherworld-mindedness into our preachers and people. Something that will make this namby-pamby, soft-handed, compromising, cringing sort of holiness as obsolete as Pharisaism was on the Day of Pentecost. Something that reveals a man's credentials by means of souls saved and sanctified and established in Christ Jesus.[4]

—J. B. Chapman
1884—1947
Editor and General Superintendent

God's Method of Carrying on His Work

I am surprised at the heartless endeavors that many of God's good people are making. They expect no results and therefore have none. They think the day of revivals is past, and for them it is. That it is hard to grapple with a lustful, pleasure-seeking, complaining, worldly people will be admitted by all, but people of strong faith will accept it as a divine challenge.

We are a revival people. We stand for holiness of heart and life and for aggressive evangelism. Such a people can never rest satisfied unless men and women are being saved and sanctified wholly.

God helping us, we mean to pay the price for its realization. And we will surely find that there is a price to pray for deep spirituality and for successful work in the soul-saving business.[5]

—H. Orton Wiley
1877—1961
Theologian and College President

The Holy Presence
Energizes Christian Service

A great fundamental heresy has entered into the Christian thinking today. It is not clear thought. Heresy is never clear—but it has come to be a conviction; it is that the divine power is not now needed for the doing of God's work. And because of this con-

viction the conditions are greatly complicated. It would be difficult to change the conditions of an army, fighting with tin
swords and living on tainted meat, if there was conviction that
they were well equipped, even though they were impotent before
the foe.

Instead of the helmet of salvation, we have wreathed our
heads with the bay tree leaves of human culture; instead of the
breastplate of righteousness, we have the popular standing with
dominant forces; instead of girding our loins with the eternal truth
of God, we are tied up with the cotton thread of higher criticism;
instead of the shield of faith, we have to discern the tide of public
opinion; instead of our feet being shod with the preparation of the
gospel until they glow with the power of God like burning brass in
a furnace, we have the shoes of human endeavor; instead of the
Sword of the Spirit—the Word of God—flashing with the fire of the
Holy Ghost, we lift the tinseled blade of human philosophy; instead of praying with all prayer and thus throwing great shells into
the enemy's camp, we are rolling balls in the alleys of worldly ambition and gain.

I would strike at the center of the whole business. What the
church needs more than anything else—its all-embracing need—is
"the promise of the Father"—the baptism with the Holy Ghost.
Whatever other churches, be they great or small, may need or ask,
the one thing for us—far above all policy, all need—is that every
one of us tarry at Jerusalem till the promise of the Father is se-
cured.[6]

—Phineas F. Bresee
1838—1915
Founding General Superintendent

Consecration Makes Us Useful

When we empty ourselves by consecration, and the refining
fire of the Lord cleanses our inmost being, we become fit places
for the Holy Spirit to indwell in His fullness. The clay of humani-

ty becomes the container of divinity. The abiding Spirit brings the grandeur of the earthen chalice to its highest dimension. In this transcendent moment our body becomes the temple of the Holy Spirit.

Our lips become His lips to speak forth His glory; our hands become His hands to reach out with a touch of healing and love; our feet become His feet to walk in the world of sorrows and burdens; our eyes become His eyes to look with compassion upon a wounded world; our personality becomes the instrument for exalting, glorifying, and magnifying the Holy Spirit.[7]

—Mendell Taylor
1912—2000
Seminary Professor

Love Sinners and Hate Sin

The unselfishness of the great majority of our people as expressed in a spirit of mercy and magnanimity has played no small part in our progress. Some have accused us of being too liberal; others have condemned us for dogmatism and narrow-mindedness. These extreme accusations are comforting, as they indicate a middle-of-the-road position. We are not liberal toward sin, and can never be, but must always show kindness and patience toward struggling human beings, and extreme liberality with our money and service. It is one thing to be liberal with wrong; another to be magnanimous with the wrongdoer. Our church has tried to be uncompromising with sin, and general in our understanding of the struggle of a fallen race. This very fact has appealed to the people, who in return have responded to our message.[8]

—General Superintendents' Quadrennial Address
to the 10th General Assembly

Holiness—Love in Action

Love is outreach. It destroys indifference, isolationism, the pride that cuts off fellowship, partiality, aloofness, exclusiveness. It must be confessed that there is a tendency among Christians to interpret holiness as withdrawal from society, civic concerns, "bad" people, and everything secular. It is true that there is in holiness this apartness; but on the other side of holiness, and saturating it to its core, is love. Holiness is self-identity; love is losing oneself in others. Holiness is wholeness; love is sharing that wholeness. Neither holiness nor love is Christian without the other. They are logically distinct but only one thing in life. It is the division of one from the other in life that distorts both. Love without holiness disintegrates into sentimentality. Personal integrity is lost. But holiness without love is not holiness at all. In spite of its label, it displays harshness, judgmentalism, a critical spirit, and all its capacity for discrimination ends in nit-picking and divisiveness.[9]

—Mildred Bangs Wynkoop
1905-97
Theologian

Well-Connected Branches Produce Fruit

As a branch is joined to the vine by natural growth, so a Christian is joined to Christ by faith. Useless and fruitless as is the branch severed from the vine, so is the Christian who does not abide in Christ. "Without me ye can do nothing" (John 15:5).

A condition for continual relation to Christ is fruitfulness. "Every branch . . . that beareth not fruit he taketh away" (v. 2). They are gathered with the wicked and cast into everlasting fire (see v. 6). There is no ground for the doctrine of eternal security here.

Fruitfulness is the result of abiding in Christ. As natural as it is for a vine to bear fruit, so it is logical for a Christian in living relation to Christ to bear the fruit of holiness within and righteous-ness without. As the vine bears grapes, those who are clean through Christ's words bear the fruit of the Spirit, which is love. The loving, obedient Christian has a redeeming influence that results in the salvation of others. This is the secret of a growing church. The fruitful branch is purged. "Now ye are clean through the word which I have spoken unto you" (v. 3), said Jesus. There is no point in arguing for either purging or pruning. Both are necessary that the fruitful branch may bring forth more fruit. The Christian whose heart is pure must be disciplined and chastened. He, accordingly, turns all his life to loving obedience to Christ the Lord. The net return to him is fullness of joy and to the Christian community healthy growth. All is to the glory of God.[10]

—G. B. Williamson
1898—1981
General Superintendent

What Love Does

Loving as Jesus loves is not "doing what comes naturally" but doing what comes supernaturally. It was natural for Him, for His very name and nature are love. But it is not natural for us whose hearts, apart from the surgery of divine grace, are selfish and stony. We can love friends and enemies alike only when "God's love has been poured into our hearts through the Holy Spirit that has been given to us" (Rom. 5:5, RSV).

Love is "the fruit of the Spirit" and is manifested in "joy, peace, patience, kindness, goodness, faithfulness, gentleness, [and] self-control" (Gal. 5:22-23, NASB). Only when self-will is crucified, and Jesus Christ reigns in our hearts unrivaled, are we able to bear the fruit of the Spirit in lavish and luscious measure. The fruit of the Spirit is a reproduction of the character traits of Christ. Only the power of the Holy Spirit is sufficient to prepare our hearts for the production of this fruit.

"The aim of our charge," said Paul, "is love that issues from a pure heart and a good conscience and sincere faith" (1 Tim. 1:5, RSV). No one can possess and express such love until the heart is pure, and only the Spirit of holiness can effect such inward cleansing. When He does, love becomes the master passion of one's life. Love determines attitudes, words, actions, and reactions.[11]

—William E. McCumber
1927-
Pastor and Editor

Serving God Spontaneously and Consistently

Nothing is much more disgusting to right-thinking people, and we think to a righteous God, than a noisy professor of religion who is fine when you can get him, but is not dependable. If he comes, he will shout, but after that he will not come for a long time. If he feels like it, he will give liberally, but his envelope is empty for 10 successive Sundays thereafter. If he feels especially like it, he will preach or testify on the street or in the jail service, but you cannot count on him to be there the next time. Spontaneity is a fine handmaid to statedliness in the worship and service of God, but it is a very faulty mistress. Serve God and worship God, spontaneously if you can, but statedly, anyhow, without regard to weather, convenience, or emotion.[12]

—J. B. Chapman
1884—1947
Editor and General Superintendent

Christian Service Stimulates Spiritual Assurance

If we keep our Lord's commandments and are faithful to our consecration vows, we shall be active Christians. Jesus says to us, "As my Father hath sent me, even so send I you" (John 20:21); "Go ye into all the world, and preach the gospel to every creature" (Mark 16:15). If we would have the continuing presence of the Spirit, we must stay around where the Spirit is at work—we must busy ourselves with the tasks of the Spirit.

It is a wise provision of a Holiness church that charges us with "seeking to do good to the bodies and souls of men; feeding the hungry, clothing the naked, visiting the sick and imprisoned, and ministering to the [sick and] needy, as opportunity and ability are given." "Pressing upon the attention of the unsaved the claims of the gospel, inviting them to the house of the Lord, and trying to compass their salvation" (the *Manual,* Church of the Nazarene, sec. 27.1 [1997—2001]).

If we are to maintain the joy and blessing of a close fellowship with the Holy Spirit, we must keep engaged in active expression of our Christian love. The Bible promises us, "And hereby we . . . shall assure our hearts before him" (1 John 3:18-19).

Does God seem far away? Am I worried as I feel for my spiritual pulse beat? I need to get out and do something for God. The exercise of Christian service will often bring deep spiritual breathing and a firm heartbeat that gives assurance of the indwelling Holy Spirit. Active Christians have little trouble with spiritual loss and uncertainty.[13]

—**A. F. Harper**
1907-
Editor

Love Shapes Effectiveness in Service

Love for God has a practical side to it. For Jesus it meant a prodigal spending of himself to save, to heal, to comfort, and to strengthen others. His own personal comforts were set aside to serve others. His own preferences were made secondary so that He might meet the needs of others.

For many, religion is just a cold, rational acceptance of a creed. Some would make it a mere sentimental attitude toward God. But Jesus taught that it must be a living, leaping flame of love that draws us into harmony with His divine will. And its practical result is that it drives us into pathways of service for Jesus.[14]

—George Coulter
1911-95
General Superintendent

Enablement for Amazing Service

If God calls you to accomplish something for Him, you can be assured He has fitted you for the task in advance. None of us is fitted for everything. There are some things of which even the cleverest of us would make an unholy mess. But "faithful is he that calleth you, who also will do it" (1 Thess. 5:24).

To turn aside from a duty God lays upon our hearts is a sin of omission. The thought of neglecting such a task is a temptation, and God does not allow temptation to come to us without also making a way to escape. Therefore sins of omission are not inevitable. Therefore we cannot properly argue that we are incapable of something to which God calls us.

Moses did try so to argue when he was called upon to remonstrate with Pharaoh. God would not be dissuaded from His purpose by Moses protesting his lack of eloquence and his inability to speak effectively to the Pharaoh, but rather proved in a miraculous manner that He could equip Moses to fulfill His purposes.[15]

—Brian L. Farmer
1934-
Pastor

God Is with Us in Our Service

One hundred and twenty came from the Upper Room. They were Spirit-filled men and women. They had received the power of the Holy Spirit. They had died to all but one thing—God's will. They had pure hearts filled with love for God and mankind. The revival started by that group swept around the world. They were walking, talking, living revivals themselves. Christ was in them, overcoming the world. Through Spirit-filled Christians and their descendants, God changed the world.

We can be encouraged, for God is with us also. We have the reality in our gospel. We preach freedom from sin and separation from the world. We lead people to an altar to repent as Christ said they must repent. We tell them to keep away from evil and to serve God. We offer the Upper Room altar, the tarrying place, and the consecration experience. These are the same, God is the same, and our world is the same.[16]

—V. H. Lewis
1912—2000
General Superintendent

Service Requires That We Pull Together

"A pull all together" will conquer anything. A united effort, and the deed is done! A shoulder-to-shoulder advance, and the battle is ours! Let us away with any spirit of overemphasized individualism. Let us thrust ecclesiastical bolshevism from our doorstep! Let us be an intelligent spiritual democracy that selects leaders because we believe in them, and then let them, as "chiefs among equals," lead us; and we will show the greatness of our hearts, the magnanimity of our spirits, by loyally adjusting ourselves to their leadership, plans, commands, and exhortations, and in that way only can we give to this generation the gospel in as full a measure as we have received it.

This pulsating, dazzling, glittering, progressful age is *ours,* if we will only banish every divisive spirit, rally every other Holiness organization and church to our side, and then, burning the bridges of retreat behind us, move forward to take the age in the name of the God of old-fashioned heart holiness! If we swing aloft the banner "No cowards need apply" and simply defy the devil and this present evil world, in the name of the virgin-born, Calvary-crucified, resurrected, ascended, and soon-coming Lord Jesus Christ, the Son of God, we can gather out in such a crusade hundreds of thousands during the next decade. We can if we will—we can and we will![17]

—J. G. Morrison
1871—1939
General Secretary of World Missions

Helpers of the Apostles

Where would the Church be without helpers? Leaders are necessary, to be sure. But leaders are limited without faithful followers.

Our first introduction to Stephen is his selection as one of seven men of good reputation, "full of the Holy Ghost and wisdom," appointed to the humble task of "[serving] tables" (Acts 6:2-3). He wasn't chosen to be an apostle, a pastor, or an evangelist. His job in the Church was to take care of its business affairs.

There isn't much glamour in being helpers. It's more exciting to be the hands on the clock than a little wheel inside, out of sight. But if one small wheel fails, the whole clock stops.

The psalmist said, "I had rather be a doorkeeper in the house of my God, than to dwell in the tents of wickedness" (Ps. 84:10). Better a servant in the Temple than a wealthy but godless sheik in his fancy tent!

Stephen proved his faithfulness in the small place and moved to larger tasks later on. But leaders and helpers alike serve One who never forgets the labor of love done for Him.[18]

—W. T. Purkiser
1910-92
Editor and College President

Creativity, Imagination, and Holiness

A living sacrifice is a vital, living person, bursting with life, impulsive, creative, individualistic, eager—with all this put at God's disposal. I would rather have a student who pesters me with questions until I'm glad when the bell rings than to try to arouse from his lethargy one who doesn't know that there are problems and would be afraid to admit their existence if he met one.

A "living sacrifice" may think some new thoughts—plan some new plans. A Luther is apt to burst out of the bondage of mediocrity and shatter precedent. A Wesley is apt to find his heart warmed again and go crashing onto a too comfortable church and stir it up. He may go running out into the fields—or into the ghettos—where a sin-saturated culture needs the well-harnessed dynamic of a Christian who cares about people. God needs people who don't quit thinking and challenging life when they become Christians. Heaven isn't here yet.[19]

—Mildred Bangs Wynkoop
1905-97
Theologian

7 ❧ "Like Him Thou Shalt Be"

Holiness Is Christlikeness—
Nothing More, Nothing Less

---※◈※---

Christ stands as the magnificent Magnet of the Christian faith. To be like Him is the noblest goal ever considered by any human being. And those of us who serve Him have a holy obsession to be like Him. But after our loftiest thoughts, our highest dreams, and our best efforts, in our own strength we always fall short of the ideal to be like Christ.

The holiness teaching of the New Testament gives us hope and inspires adventure. It promises a holy, inner power that draws and enables us to become more and more like Him. Try applying this holy promise to your own faith journey: "God knew what he was doing from the very beginning. He decided from the outset to shape the lives of those who love him along the same lines as the life of his Son. The Son stands first in the line of humanity he restored. We see the original and intended shape of our lives there in him" (Rom. 8:29, TM).

A few lines from a masterful sermon by Paul Rees draw me onward in my quest to be like Jesus: "You ask me to define the love of God. I can't, but I can point you to Jesus: He is it. You ask me to define the grace of God that forgives sin, and reshapes lives, and purifies character. I can't, but I can point you to Jesus: He is it. You ask me to define the power of God by which the weak are made strong, and the dead are raised up, and by which, one day, all the divine purposes will be fulfilled. I can't, but I can point you to Jesus. He is it."[1]

That's it—"He is it." And He has captured my heart and my will forever. That fascination with Jesus is at the heart of Holiness teaching and the adventure of living a holy life.

—Neil B. Wiseman

Christ—Our First Loyalty

Christ should have first priority over our personalities, our potentialities, our possessions, and our pleasures. He is my Sovereign and I am His subject. He is the first cause, fixed center, full circumference, and final consummation of all my aspirations and anticipations. My time, my talents, and my tithe are all at His disposal. Putting Christ first, we do not minor on majors or major on minors, but we place incidental things in an incidental place and fundamental realities in the fundamental place. First things are always first in our hearts and lives.

Christ is unexcelled, unsurpassed, unequaled, unparalleled, incomparable, transcendent, and superlative! How could a redeemed soul ever place Him in any other position than first? He belongs first. He will be first. This Emperor has an empire. This King has a kingdom. As trees outgrow twigs, as rivers outflow rills, as suns outshine sparks, as oceans outsweep dewdrops, as seranading seraphims outsing chirping crickets, so the kingdom of God towers above all other kingdoms of earth. How could a true follower of Christ place His kingdom in any other plan than first? If you place Christ first, you will place His cause first. He will be Ruler over your all, or He will not be your Ruler at all. His kingdom will have our first loyalty.

Everything and everybody will be secondary, and He must be primary and preeminent. He will rule and reign from center to circumference, throughout every crack, crevice, and corner, without rival or reservation, as King of Kings and Lord of Lords, high over all, now and forevermore. "Seek ye the kingdom of God; and all these things shall be added unto you" (Luke 12:31).[2]

—Paul J. Stewart
1912-87
Evangelist and Pastor

Unlimited Spiritual Growth in Christlikeness

A sanctified man is at the bottom of the ladder. He is but a child—a clean child. He is now to learn, to grow, to rise, to be divinely enlarged and transformed. The Christ in him is to make new and complete channels in and through every part of his being—pouring the stream of heaven through his thinking, living, devotion, and faith.[3]

—Phineas F. Bresee
1838—1915
Founding General Superintendent

What Does Spirituality Mean?

We are likely to want to define spirituality in terms of emotion, zeal, or demonstration; but these are mere incidentals, as much the product of natural human temperament as of divine power. Spirituality is more fundamental than any or all of them. . . .

To be truly spiritual is to be holy in the innermost center and core of the personality. This requires the purification of the thoughts of the mind and of the imaginations of the heart and the bringing of all the ransomed powers of body, soul, and spirit under the influence and direction of the Holy Spirit. Spirituality is more, even, than communion with God, for it is the communication of God to us in such a manner as to make us truly "partakers of the divine nature" (1 Pet. 1:4). It is emphatically "Christ crowned within." It is the state of one who has found his home in God and in whom God has truly found a place of abiding.

Before one can be truly "spiritual," he must meet all the conditions for reconciliation with God. He must comply with the requirements for communion with God. He must press on into that intimate acquaintance with God that makes him truly "conscious," as well as "confident," of God, and he must become so pliable as to qualify as a channel through which God can be revealed.[4]

—J. B. Chapman
1884—1947
Editor and General Superintendent

You Have Me—I Am Enough

I have often read of that night of darkness and loneliness, of weeping and prayer, in the life of Dr. Bresee, when in order to carry out his commission to preach full salvation to the poor he was to all intents and purposes dropped from the ministry of the church to which he had given so many years of service. He loved that church; his friends were there; the ministers who had been his dearly beloved brethren were all there—but now, these were his no longer. He could find help only in prayer and tears.

I have heard him say that, driving along in his buggy one day, he passed a new building in process of erection. Satan said to him, "You could have a building like this, the best churches in the denomination, if you would cease to preach along certain lines."

In the midst of that darkness and oppression, Jesus whispered softy to him and said, "You have Me."

From out of that dark cave of doubt and desertion, there issued the beginnings of what has become a great church—men and women who stand firmly for the peace of God imparted by the Holy Spirit—and a church that is rapidly reaching out to the ends of the earth with the gospel of full salvation.[5]

—H. Orton Wiley
1877—1961
Theologian and College President

Like Jesus—the Strength of Meekness

Moses, while in the school of God, was not brought to an attitude of meekness in a day. God did not extinguish the flaming passion in Moses that slew the Egyptian; He harnessed it to lofty purposes by stripping it of its savagery. It is absurd to deplore the possession of a fiery temper; when God sanctifies it, it becomes infinitely valuable.

Meekness is not a sign of weakness, but of well-governed strength. Many a man who refuses to be infuriated under rebuke is misjudged for lack of spirit; in truth, he displays more strength of character by his spiritual poise in knowing how to possess his vessel. "He that is slow to anger is better than the mighty; and he that ruleth his spirit than he that taketh a city" (Prov. 16:32).

To be meek does not mean that one has a backbone like a jellyfish. Jesus, who was meekest of all, did not hesitate to manifest His strength and courage in defense of right and the punishment of wrong, neither will He. For desecrating the house of God Jesus overthrew the tables of the money changers and drove them from the Temple with a scourge of small cords. Yet He had the meek poise of character to return a smile for a frown and a blessing for a curse.

The first beatitude requires humiliation, while the third demands of us humility. But the meek have the promise even of an earthly inheritance that is above their fellows—"They shall inherit the earth" (Matt. 5:5).[6]

—Fred M. Weatherford
d. 1980
Pastor

Friendship with Jesus

If you ran out of bread in the desert, He would take a few loaves and have more bread than you needed. If you fell sick and there weren't any hospitals near, Jesus would take care of that by healing you. If there wasn't any boat, He could walk the water. And if the government stuck on some extra tax and you were broke, He could tell you where to land a tax-fish. What a Person to have for your Friend.

Yes, it seems wonderful. But there was a catch to it. You had some responsibilities if He was going to be your Friend. "You are My friends if you do [the things which] I command you"! (John 15:14, NKJV). Ah, there it was. And, what are the commandments? Well, there are many of them. "Love one another" (v. 17, NKJV). "Deny [yourself], and take up [your] cross" (Matt. 16:14, NKJV).

Oh, we want to fellowship with Christ at Cana where the water turns to wine, and in the desert where the bread is multiplied—and in heaven. But we don't like joining the church at Golgotha, do we? But Paul caught the idea: "That I may know Him . . . and the fellowship of His sufferings" (Phil. 3:10, NKJV). Paul wanted to be a comrade to Calvary. He wanted to join Christ at the Cross. That is real friendship.

We are not really Christ's best friends because we are intimate with His Canas and His Bethanys—we must be intimate with His Calvarys.[7]

—Lon Woodrum
1901-95
Evangelist

What Jesus Is like and How Can We Be Like Him

The Bible teaches a lot about Jesus and about what we can become:

1. He is eternal. He existed before worlds were created, for He had a hand in their creation. He will never cease to exist.

2. He is divine. He is God, a member of the Trinity. He is as divine as if He had never become a human being.

3. He was human. He was as much a human being as if He had never been divine. He was two complete, whole natures in one—the God-Man.

4. He was divinely conceived of the Holy Ghost and born of the Virgin Mary. His mother was a human being; His Father was God.

5. He died, not as a martyr, not as a misunderstood fanatic, but vicariously, paying the price for the redemption of the human race. He died to save me from my sins. To save you from your sins.

6. He arose from the tomb, conquering death. The angel who rolled the stone away did not awake Him from death. Nor did the angel roll away the stone to let Him out of the tomb. Jesus was already risen from the grave before the stone was rolled away. His resurrection was an essential part of the scheme to redeem us.

7. He ascended into heaven. Jesus said He would do this. What if He had stayed on earth, making tours that we may see Him once in a lifetime? Christianity would have been vastly different.

8. He is coming soon. This is His promise, and the signs are pointing, as He said. He could return today. He may!

9. He demands some things of the sinner: a complete repentance, a turning from sin, a new birth, a perfect obedience.

10. He demands some things of the saint: that we press on into holiness; that we be faithful in our service; that we tell this blessed story everywhere and constantly until He comes again.[8]

—Fletcher Spruce
1913-74
Pastor and District Superintendent

Our Pattern for Living: What Would Jesus Do?

When wildly beat the storms of life,
With thunderclouds of hate and strife;
*   When roads are rough and friends are few,*
*   Then whisper, "What would Jesus do?"*

When you are called to take the road
Of sacrifice, and bear the load,

Where fields are white—the workers few,
Consider, "What would Jesus do?"
When fierce temptations round you sweep,
While friends you trusted scoff or sleep;
  When truth and right are lost to view,
  Ask bravely, "What would Jesus do?"

O let Him guide and pattern be,
Heed His soft whisper—"Follow me,"
  For surely He will take you through
  While praying, "What would Jesus do?"'

—Kathryn Blackburn Peck
c. 1904-75
Poet and Children's Editor

Christlike Use of Power

When power is conferred upon one, is there not an *obligation, a debt,* conferred with it? When office comes to a man, we recognize that he is obligated to use its influence for the Master. When riches come, we insist that a stern stewardship applies to their use. By what sort of reasoning, then, can we escape the inexorable law of the stewardship of prayer?

Power unused is soon forfeited. The blacksmith's arm unexercised withers. The brain unemployed grows flabby and nonproductive. The prayerless believer speedily becomes the powerless believer. Unmindful of prayer's dynamics, we cease its frequent exercise, and soon it means little more than so much pious human pattering. Through disuse it has lost its divine force.

Think you we shall not be called to account for our stewardship of the amazing potencies of prayer? Will not the Judgment Day reveal the marching lines of lost souls, hell bound because we did not pray? Will not churches unmoved as they might have been moved, had we made determined intercession for them, rise up to witness against our faithless stewardship in that awful day? Will not our own flesh and blood, wandered from paths of righteousness because of prayerless parents, haunt with staring eyes our path to the Judgment. Will not graceless ages, sunk in sin, loom big with condemnation when we see how changed they might have been if we had prayed?

We owe it, then; it is a debt divinely required, that all "men pray every where, lifting up holy hands, without wrath and doubting" (1 Tim. 2:8). "[Pray] always with all . . . supplication" (Eph. 6:18), Paul the apostle says.[10]

—J. G. Morrison
1871—1939
General Secretary of World Missions

Unclaimed Deposits of Grace

More than a quarter of a century ago I was riding with a gentleman through the leading business street of Cleveland. Suddenly he pointed to a noble granite bank building, 11 stories high, and said, "That building was built by the interest on unclaimed deposits in that bank." Why did not the rightful owners of such vast sums of money claim it? Evidently they did not know that it belonged to them. Why was it?

A few illustrations will make it plain. First, we may suppose, a young unmarried man whose home is a thousand miles away, or perhaps in England or Scotland or Germany, is doing business in Cleveland and making large deposits in that bank when suddenly he dies. His faraway relatives never hear of the wealth, and the bank officials never divulge the secret. Another businessman, secretive about his financial affairs and whose wife is inclined to be too extravagant, uses two banks. One bank he uses daily in his transactions, as his wife knows. In this other bank we are writing about, he makes his permanent deposits and has his private papers in a safety-deposit drawer, of which his wife knows absolutely nothing. He dies suddenly out of his mind. The wife settles with the other much-used bank as best she can; but of the larger deposits in the other bank, she is perfectly ignorant, and the officials are mum. Now in the case of an old and powerful bank, there may come to be hundreds or even thousands of such instances of unclaimed deposits, and the rightful heirs, ignorant of these facts, may have lived in penury and died in want.

Now, our Elder Brother, Jesus Christ, has made vast deposits of grace in the bank of heaven for us all, enough to make us all spiritual millionaires! The difference between this bank and that bank in Cleveland is this: the bank of heaven is perpetually advertising these deposits in a little black Book called the Bible, which has an immense circulation. It also sends out agents (evangelists) all over the world to herald the glad news, that poverty-stricken sinners may inherit millions of grace from God.[11]

—A. M. Hills
1848—1951
• **Theologian and College President**

━━◆━━

Jesus—the Perfect Picture of God

Christ is the Light of the World. He is the Source of all the knowledge we have of the Divine Being—His relation to us, His infinite love for us, and His wonderful plan of salvation for us. He is the Source of all our hope, our peace, our comfort, and our assurance. He is the Source of all the knowledge we have of our home beyond, of the many mansions and the place prepared for us.

Christ is the "Light, which lighteth every man that cometh into the world" (John 1:9). One has said that the idea of God is a Lighted Lamp hung up in the dome of every man's soul as he comes into the world.

Man, created in God's own image, can find satisfaction only in God. The idea or awareness of God, like a dim twinkle of a little lamp in the soul, drives men in heathen lands where the True Light has never shined to make gods of wood and stone, clay, paper, or rags and give to these false gods fanatical devotion.

Christ is the True Light. He is the perfect Mirror of God's unfathomable love to all men, and you and I are ordained to be the reflectors of that Light, "[even] unto the uttermost part of the earth" (Acts 1:8).[12]

—Louise R. Chapman
1892—1993
Missionary and President of Nazarene World Mission Society

Jesus' New Perspective

Jesus shocked people by giving morals a new dimension. He talked of murderers who had killed nobody, thieves who had stolen nothing, and adulterers who had never experienced physical excursion into extramarital intimacy. He said they had "looked to lust" (see Matt. 5:28) and in so doing had adulterated their own morals. He recognized that it was possible for our lives and our institutions to be adulterated by inner corruption without violating any of the laws of men. He knew that the real adulterating of the life began in the inner person.

He who adulterates himself adulterates also the institutions that enclose him. He who cheapens the nobility of his inner soul has deprived his marriage and marriage partner of something the other has a right to possess. He who diminishes his own worth robs the mate who loves him, the children who have a right to his best, and the society that needs to see his finest stature.[13]

—Milo L. Arnold
1903-87
Pastor

Deliverance Is Coming

To look at the saints in this world one can see that it hath not been revealed what they shall be. They are scarred, marred, infirm, old, failing, fading, poor, crippled, wrinkled, decrepit. They die like all others; they suffer like all mankind. They are tempted and troubled on every hand. The work of the devil has shown itself in their bodies and minds. But deliverance is coming. They shall be like Him. Not one thing that sin and Satan has marred them with shall be left on them when He transforms them into His likeness. They shall see Him as He is, because they believed on Him as He was in this world. Being made like unto Him by His grace shall assure them that they shall be like unto Him in His glory. "For this purpose the Son of God was manifested, that he might destroy the works of the devil" (1 John 3:8).[14]

—T. M. Anderson
1888—1929
Pastor and Evangelist

The Rocklike Qualities of Holiness

Peter is like so many of us—or like our notions of ourselves—that we are somehow willing to stand or fall with him. Winsome, whole-souled, transparent Peter—surely you will make it through. What are your assets?

Sincere—yet when faced with startling, overwhelming danger and disappointment Peter dissembles and lies outright. Fearless—yet suddenly and surprisingly he finds himself a moral coward. Ready of speech—he uses his tongue foolishly, heedlessly, inquisitively, boastfully, even profanely. Quick to apprehend the truth—he is as quick to cast it away when he cannot understand the present circumstance. Loving Jesus truly and confident of his own love—he cannot trust in the dark; he forgets so soon. Is this Peter, or is it me? I, too, mean well always, but there is a streak of quicksand in me somewhere.

Peter finally makes it. The quicksand layer is removed, and solid rock takes its place. I, too, must experience this transformation; or I shall sometime prove a bitter disappointment to myself, to those who have confidence in me, and to my Lord.[15]

—Bertha Munro
1887—1983
Educator

Consecration—Doing Yourself a Favor

It is not our love of sin and the world we are giving up, but our love of ourselves. In repentance we abandon the *bad,* but in consecration we surrender the *good.* This touches our inherent right to ourselves. This is not dealing with evil practices but with God's gifts. "Why should we give them up?" we whimper. Yet this and nothing less is the biblical challenge: "I beseech you therefore, brethren, by the mercies of God, that ye present your bodies a living sacrifice, holy, acceptable unto God, which is your reasonable service" (Rom. 12:1). Most Christians find that it is far easier to give up sins than to give up self. In this struggle the carnal mind feels that God is asking too much.

It is for this reason that making a thorough and honest consecration generally requires a little time. Not that any emphasis should ever be placed on the time factor, as if there were any virtue or necessity in so many hours of seeking or so much fasting. But the soul does need a deep view of its own corruption. It does need to count the cost. It does need to specify the items of yielding—money, job, family, ambitions, affections, reputation, success or failure, occupation, the present or the future, the "known bundle" and the "unknown bundle" (as old-timers used to call it). We must genuinely come to grips with practical personal, down-to-earth issues that bother us. What if God should . . . ? Yes, we must face *that* possibility, until we are able to say, "Not my will, but thine, be done" (Luke 22:42). In this process we see that God's will may cut across the natural. Then the natural must be surrendered. The ego must be slain. The *Big I* must be crucified.[16]

—Richard S. Taylor
1912-
Theologian and Seminary Professor

What Is Carnality?

Carnality dims the vision, circumscribes the horizon, dulls the expectation, defeats the prayer life, and keeps the heart cold and indifferent toward the dying thousands who without God and without hope in the world are slipping to eternal ruin.

Carnality counts the cost—the pure in heart count God. Carnality is man-fearing—the sanctified are God-fearing. Carnality is self-centered—a pure heart is God-centered. Carnality has many interests—a pure heart is single in its aim and vision. Carnality is the source and spirit of the blight of ordinariness that damns and curses the Church and the world by inaction. The great modern church with its culture, brains, and money has either gone out of the soul-saving business or misplaced it by methods to reach and draw people to the church. In either case the soul-passion is lacking, and the Holy Spirit, indwelling a pure heart, is soul-passion. Carnality is never anxious for the conversion of lost souls and the purifying of believers to the extent of prayer, sacrifice, and giving. . . . The objective of carnality in a believer is to misdirect the purpose of the believer and to kill with the blight of ordinariness the very purpose itself.[17]

—Howard W. Jerrett
c. 1884—1967
Pastor

The Life That Pleases God

The Lord is really greatly pleased when His people really trust Him and grieved when they don't. That's the core of the pleasure of God found in Enoch, Noah, Abraham, Paul, and the others; they *trusted Him!* They took Him at His word, acted on His naked promise, and gambled their lives that He meant every syllable He spoke. They stuck out their necks in the trust that actually He is much greater than even His promises.

Oh, but God likes that! He is grieved by our caution, our calculating reluctance and tardiness of trust, because a lack of trust is a vote of no confidence in our Heavenly Father. God gets great joy in them that trust Him (Rom. 4:19-25).

The life that pleases God is not to be measured by its length of years, nor even by its breadth of interest; it is measured by its depths. The Lord loves those who look to the roots, digging deep and growing roots on their souls, roots that thrust themselves toward the river of His life. Life in the Spirit is like climbing a clean mountain; life in the flesh is like rummaging in a back alley lined with garbage bins into which we toss our most precious possibilities. Life in the Spirit is life in God's third dimension. It has eyes that see the invisible, ears that hear the inaudible, hands that grasp the intangible.

Rom. 12:1 clinches that: "Think of God's mercy, my brothers, and worship him, I beg you, . . . by offering your living bodies as a holy sacrifice, truly pleasing to God" (JB). That really pleases God; He is looking for people like that (John 4:23). Spiritual worship is the offering of my life in sanctified service. He who would live for God's pleasure must, like Jesus, be "numbered with the transgressors" (Isa. 53:12) and become the servant of all!

It is the lifestyle of the entirely sanctified. This life cannot be lived with sin in the heart. God hates sin and would root and rout it out of our hearts. Jesus said so: "Every plant, which my heavenly Father hath not planted, shall be rooted up" (Matt. 15:13). Sin of every sort, and all sorts, is the work of the devil; Jesus came to destroy that (1 John 3:8). God intends His people to be clean, free from sin, and possessed by the Spirit of holiness. We must please God (1 Thess. 2:4). It is not ultimately imperative that we please anyone else, although we do not desire to displease others. But we absolutely must please God; and as Paul says, we must learn to do so more and more.

To live the life that pleases God is not merely a high ideal, something beyond the possible. It is the highest ideal, but it is offered to God's children in grace. "Offered"—spell it out slowly, letting the letters drip into your soul. The holy life is the life that gives God pleasure; therefore all the riches of His grace and power are open to turn His promises into experience. Kinship and empathy at base lie in oneness of interest and aim. The apostle Peter shows us that God's great command to be holy is really an evangelical promise to make us so: "You shall be holy, for I am holy" (1 Pet. 1:16, AMP, NEB, RSV; cf. NASB). "But just as he who called you is holy, so be holy in all you do" (v. 15, NIV). The measure of the "so" is the measure of the corresponding "as."[18]

—T. Crichton Mitchell
1916-96
Pastor and Educator

8 ❋ "Thy Friends in Thy Conduct His Likeness Shall See"

How Do Holy People Behave?

Our parents and grandparents believed the inner work of holiness showed in their outward conduct. They practiced holiness in every dimension of their living. What I saw in them is summarized in the soul-searching prayer from Mother Teresa of Calcutta:

"Dear Lord, help me to spread thy fragrance everywhere I go. Flood my soul with thy spirit and life. Penetrate and possess my whole being so utterly that all my life may only be a radiance of thine. Shine through me, and be so in me that every soul I come in contact with may feel thy presence in my soul. . . .

"Let me preach thee without preaching, not by words but by my example, by the catching force, the sympathetic influence of what I do, the evident fullness of the love my heart bears to thee. Amen."[1]

—Neil B. Wiseman

Real Love Shows in Conduct

Let the heart be opened to the incoming of the baptism of perfect love, and it will expel everything else. Every man who loves God with all his heart will love his neighbor as himself. He will no longer be envious of another's prosperity but, rather, rejoice in every man's success. He will cherish no hatred nor malice. He will be grieved and distressed at another's misfortune.

Christian love delights not to get but to give. As someone has defined, it is the giving impulse. So that far from grudging the good things that come to another, it rejoices in them. Envy is selfish. Love is the exact antithesis of all that. In its very nature it is unselfish and sacrificial. As love takes possession of the soul, this ugly and bitter affection disappears from the life.

The heart filled with Christian love is intent, not on getting goods, but on doing good. Like the pilgrims in *Vanity Fair* it lifts its eyes from the glittering prizes of earth and has its trade and traffic in heaven and buys only the truth.[2]

—A. S. London
1887—1974
Sunday School Evangelist

The Surprise of Serving and Giving

Unselfish giving never results in poverty. Happy is that individual who early in Christian service cultivates the grace of giving. In a short time the harvest will be remarkably increased.

Life is too short in years and too full of eternal values to be wasted. It cannot be weighed on scales used for weighing gold or silver. A friendly smile, a warm handclasp, or an encouraging word may help some neighbor or friend over a difficult path. Men do not often talk of their problems. Today we may meet one of God's children carrying a heartbreaking load. Let us share with him the manifold blessings that God has given us. While telling others of God's goodness, we will be able not only to help lighten their load but also to find grace anew for our own hearts.

Everyone pities a physical dwarf. How startling would be the sight if professors of religion should show in physical stature their exact spiritual growth and attainment! What a surprising sight if we should see persons who have recorded their spiritual birth many years ago and are still in their infancy. Christians grow as they share with others. Lord, help me to carry another's load today; then my own burden will well-nigh be forgotten.[3]

—Bertha Mae Lillenas
1889—1945
Songwriter

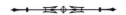

You Have a Bright Future with God

After Abraham had answered the call of God to leave his family and land of his youth to go to the place that he should afterward receive for an inheritance, he found there was strife between the herdsmen of Lot's cattle and his own herdsmen. By mutual agreement they consented to separate. Abraham the elder gave Lot the younger the privilege of choice, and he chose the well-watered plains of Jordan, which left to Abraham the hills and broadening fields.

After the separation of Lot from Abraham, God appeared unto him upon the mountaintop asking him to "lift up now thine eyes, and look from the place where thou art northward, and southward, and eastward, and westward: for all the land which thou seest, to thee will I give it" (Gen. 13:14-15). This marked an epoch in the life of Abraham; it was to him the mount of broadened vision of what God had called him away from his father's house to enjoy.

Abraham is not the only child of God who has stood on the mount of broadened vision. God is calling all His children to go with Him to this mount to see what their privileges in Christ Jesus are. He has not called us out from among the world of sinners, with their folly, their iniquity, their fellowships, their pleasures, merely to be a separated people. He has called us out that we may explore the land of spiritual realities now opened to us.[4]

—D. Shelby Corlett
1867—1954
Editor

Faith Rewarded Now and Forever

There is a thirst for life from deep within the soul of man. As Pilgrim ran for the wicket gate crying "Life! Life! Eternal life!" so the soul cries out for life that never ends. The fight of the body against physical death is an object lesson in the desire of the whole man for life. The longing of the soul in the depths of its most quiet moment is for a life with the restrictions of time and physical limitations removed.

In the early centuries of the Christian Church, a sentence to labor in the salt mines of Numidia was a sentence to death. It was comparable to a sentence to a Siberian slave-labor camp. And yet on the walls of the salt mines the word most often inscribed was "vita"—"life." In the midst of the living death was the thirst for life.

But God's promise is qualitative as well as quantitative. It has to do with the nature of our living as well as its duration. All men will continue to exist eternally, but all will not have eternal life. For some there will be eternal death. When Jesus promised eternal life to men who would accept Him, He was not making some immortal and others destined to end with the grave. He was talking about the kind of living that brought life and life more abundant. Eternal life in that sense can begin here on earth. Death will remove the restrictions of physical existence and will bring the glorious fulfillment of what was begun on earth.

Is the life I now live worthy of being perpetuated eternally? If I were God, would I want such a person as I, with a life like mine, to live on eternally? Eternal life is based on our relationship with Jesus Christ, whom to know aright is life eternal.[5]

—W. Shelburne Brown
1918-78
Pastor and Educator

The Holy Strength of Simple Things

If you and I seek the great towering experiences as our path to completeness, we miss the mark. There cannot be many towering experiences. If they multiply, they cease to be towering. We need to find a way to find experiences that bless a moment, then fill many moments with them. It must be what we are doing in the here and now that will become the rewarding ingredient of our lifetime.

Our challenge and call may be to the simple life of hoeing weeds, washing pots and pans, or the giving of a cup of cold water to a thirsting stranger.[6]

—Milo L. Arnold
1903-87
Pastor

In Our Living—
Light Always Threatens Darkness

The coming of Jesus into a darkened world was the coming of light. His approach to men individually is the coming of light to a darkened soul. The coming of light anywhere, at any time, is an event both glorious and dangerous. It is glorious in that it is something from the heart of God himself, destined to deliver, to help, and to bless. It is dangerous because, unless the soul is prepared to accept it, to walk in its rays and to obey its dictates and implications, there are reactions that leave tragic scars. That soul can never be the same again. Light received illumines, blesses, and transforms, while light rejected will blight, sear, and leave a trail of death.

The world in its sin did not want the God-sent light, beneficent though it was intended to be, and at Calvary did its best to extinguish it. In that moment the world put itself into a deeper darkness than ever it had known before, and yet the light it had sought to put out only shone with a more radiant glow.

I must be careful what I do with light. New spiritual light will come to me as I go along. I can never be the same again after I have faced it. I may trifle with it and even profess a broadening of views, but in my heart of hearts I know that I can never un-see any truth I have really seen. Let me walk in the light; it will pay me best.[7]

—Harry E. Jessop
1884—1974
Writer and Evangelist

Strength for Every Situation

There are many great and gracious promises in the Bible and even in this chapter, but this exceeds them all: "And as thy days, so shall thy strength be" (Deut. 33:25).

First, it is a general promise. "Our days," "all our days," "our days from the cradle to the grave." The writer is an old man in years and much older in experience. His life has been a strange one—born in a crucial period, abandoned by his folk when a babe, and committed to a basket out on the river Nile. A princess came to bathe, saw the basket, had a slave go for it, uncovered the cargo, and behold, it was a Hebrew baby. He pelted her with his tears and cries until her better self arose and she took him to her bosom as her own. The angels watched the scene, and when a nurse was called, it was his own mother; who could better train a boy than his own godly mother?

Forty years he spent in a heathen palace and court. Forty years he beheld an idolatrous people and saw the vice and corruption of this people. Forty years his soul hated the evils of the land. He spent 40 years now on the backside of a desert in God's school, being prepared for his 40 years of lifework. God did, through this man, lead His people from bondage. And as he now rehearses the Law and God's dealing with Israel to this young generation, he cries, "As thy days, so shall thy strength be."

It may be a sunshiny day when all is bright, or it may be a very dark and cloudy day. There are days of sunshine, and there are cloudy days in the lives of all. It may be a day of prosperity, or it may be a day of adversity. It may be one of those days when we quote, "[Stand], and having done all, . . . stand" (Eph. 6:13). To even "stand" in that day is to have gained the victory. It may be a day when the postman brings cheering news of the well-being of distant loved ones. Again it may be a day when we receive a shocking message telling of the death of someone very dear to our hearts. It may be a day when the flood tides of glory sweep over our souls, or it may be one of those lean days when it seems that God is afar off. Those are the days that are hard to understand. Whatever it may be, God be praised that we can still shout, "As thy days, so shall thy strength be."[8]

—H. H. Wise
1889—1948
Pastor

⟡

Reckless Faith for Fulfilled Living

Faith quickens the powers of vision of the soul. It intensifies the depths of sight to behold the unseen. It pierces the temporal and material and looks through the veil of time into eternity. It enabled Abraham to see the better country and to push toward the city of God. Even while dwelling in tents in a changeable world he was able, by the eye of faith, to live in the world that is changeless and eternal. This vision enabled him to make all of his decisions in the light of the eternal. He saw the covenant of God superior and more lasting than any earthly relation.

Isaac also had the vision of faith and counted the covenant more lasting than his generation, for he "blessed Jacob and Esau concerning things to come" (Heb. 11:20).

Joseph, too, was able to look by the eye of faith beyond his day and believe that God would fulfill His covenant to the fathers. His faith was so strong and constant that he "made mention of the departing of the children of Israel; and gave commandment concerning his bones" (v. 22).

Faith's vision enabled the prophets to give God's message regarding future things. It gave courage to the apostles to evangelize the world of their day. It was the source of courage to the martyrs of the past, and it has given stimulation unto multitudes in the daily grind of routine life.

Faith has guided and will continue to guide the Christian to look for the "more exceeding and eternal weight of glory" (2 Cor. 5:17). The Man of Galilee needs followers today who will exercise the recklessness of faith. The challenge is being thrown out to all disciples to come out of the crowd, to break with the indifference of the age, to arise from the lethargy settling on the Church, and to go forth as a knight of the burning heart—striving by the passion of love and with dauntless courage—to go forth as an example of spiritual victory today.

God's grace is sufficient. His promises are true. He will verify His Word. He will give constant victory to all who will answer the challenge of faith.[9]

—Lewis T. Corlett
1896–1992
Seminary President

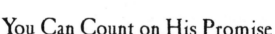

You Can Count on His Promise

There are a vast number of promises recorded in the Word of God. Most of them are conditional. By that we mean that we cannot hope to realize their fulfillment unless certain conditions are met. "If we confess our sins, he is faithful and just to forgive us" (1 John 1:9). "Trust in the LORD, and do good; so shalt thou dwell in the land, and verily thou shalt be fed" (Ps. 37:3). "If ye abide in me, and my words abide in you, ye shall ask what ye will, and it shall be done unto you" (John 15:7).

It cannot be said that all things work together for good to those who are aliens to the grace of God, to those who reject His mercies, who seek their own pleasures and are children of the world. The promise is given only to those who love God. Remember, then, through all the perplexing problems of life, in all the unforeseen situations you encounter, that your Heavenly Father has so planned it that all things will work together for your good.[10]

—Haldor Lillenas
1885—1959
Pastor and Songwriter

The Whole Self Centered in God Shows in the Details

"Bless the LORD, O my soul: and *all* that is within me, bless his holy name" (Ps. 103:1, italics added). What a symphony of praise. This is the highest good in life sought by sage and philosopher and human prophet in vain, but found in the sanctified heart cleansed by the power of the Blood and kept clean by the power of an endless life.

What a blissful state of the soul when in answer to the eternal question "What is man's highest good, his fullest duty, the realization of his greatest powers?" the whole symphony of the heart responds, "To know God and to glorify Him forever"—when

The eye answers, "My highest good is to see God's face."

The ear responds, "My highest good is to hear God's voice."

The tongue asserts, "My highest good is to announce God's praises."

The sensibilities agree, "Our highest good is to feel Him nigh."

The memory affirms, "My highest good is to be filled with the recollections of His grace."

The imagination replies, "My highest good is to contemplate the future in His will."

The reason pronounces, "My highest good is to know God and His Son, Jesus Christ."

The emotions declare, "Our highest good is to love God and love as He loves."

The will proclaims, "My highest good is to obey God and realize His purpose for me."

Thus from the entire soul as from a great symphony orchestra the single theme played by the full instrumentation of the soul is this complete harmony within, and agreement with the heart and nature of the Creator of the soul. *This* is holiness of heart.[11]

—Floyd W. Nease
1893—1930
Educator

Holiness—a Wonderful Way of Living

Sanctification is an act and a life. It is a crisis and a process. It is a doctrine, but it is doctrine in shoe leather, as well as on the books. Its beauty is not mainly in words, for words apart from vital living condemn it. Its loveliness and power are in a life lived out by the grace of God.

Holiness can never be accepted, intellectually, merely as a philosophy of life. It turns gangrenous apart from the constant flow of living blood out of a pure heart. Sanctification does not provide character in a nice, neat bundle at an altar, but it clears the ground for character building and remains as a vital relationship to God so long as the recipient continues to work the ground.

Holiness means something. It means everything. It means a beginning, but it also means a continuing. Even more than that, it means a constantly augmented enlargement of love commensurate with the daily growth of human personality. It may begin in a small soul, but no soul can remain small and retain it. It may begin in promises, but it dies apart from the fulfillment of the promises that involve the stewardship of personality development.[12]

—Mildred Bangs Wynkoop
1905-97
Theologian

The Adventure of This Holy Journey

Purity is subtraction, and it is instantaneously accomplished. Maturity is addition. It is the result of experience, trial, conflict, nutrition. In my youth I watched the workmen, at a given time in the spring, spray the peach trees to kill the insects, the worms, the "impurity." But it took many weeks of warm sunshine to produce the luscious, ripe peaches.

Thus entire sanctification is not merely the negative goodness of a cleansing of the heart wrought at the moment of faith but also the aggressive and progressive living, growing, maturing; the applying of the principles of Christian ethics to every part of the life, "till we all come in the unity of the faith, and of the knowledge of the Son of God, unto a perfect man, unto the measure of the stature of the fulness of Christ" (Eph. 4:13).

A steamship line carries the slogan "Half the fun is getting there." Half the fun of heaven can be "getting there" with a life of holiness down here.[13]

—William E. McCumber
1927-
Pastor and Editor

Walk with Christ in Good Works

Before a man or woman can walk in good works, he or she must be re-created in Christ Jesus by the transforming power of His Spirit.

Good works are the consequences of salvation, not the means or the cause. But these consequences will always follow the cause. So you may know beyond a doubt whether a person has been transformed by the grace of God by the *fruits* of his living.

Now good works are lovely. They are things done in conformity to the will of God. There must be an orthodoxy of the heart and life as well as of the mind. I am afraid of a man who claims to be sound on his understanding of the Atonement but remains a bit shady in his character, for Christianity demands that orthodoxy of creed must always issue in orthopraxy of conduct. Belief without works is dead (see James 3:20). Creed without conduct is dead also. And always the worth of an action is contingent upon its motive.

Paul urgently emphasizes the necessity of walking in good works by reference to the fact that such a walk has been ordained beforehand by God for everyone who has become the recipient of His marvelous grace. The consistent walk of the Christian in the things of godliness is the crowning proof that we are God's workmanship. Do you bear the marks of the nail-pierced hands?[14]

—Ross E. Price
1907-
Educator and Pastor

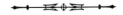

Victorious Living

In this great struggle against sin and wrongdoing there is little to remind us daily of the fight. There are no bursting bombs, no roaring of artillery as the big guns belch forth death upon the enemy. But the warfare is nevertheless real.

Paul, one of the early soldiers of the Cross, said, "We wrestle not against flesh and blood, but against principalities, against powers, . . . against spiritual wickedness in high places" (Eph. 6:12). In this fight there are no exemptions for everyone who names the name of Christ. There are battles to be fought.

In order to win as a Christian in the fight against sin and wrongdoing we must make a consecration, not just for time and space but wide enough and deep enough to embrace all eternity. Then like Paul we must "[be true] to the heavenly vision" (Acts 26:19). This calls for a wholehearted devotion to Christ and His Church. Whatever the sacrifices may be, we must accept them gladly.

Genuine Christians only ask, "What is God's will for me?" and once they know, ever afterward that is their delight.[15]

—A. L. Parrott
1891—1976
Pastor and Educator

The Miracle of Memory

Memory is to the individual what history is to the human race. Can you imagine how helpless a person would be without memory? Without it he would be utterly feebleminded and incapable of profiting from his previous experiences.

But some things are best forgotten! It is well that we cannot recall the losses, bitter sorrows, and searing wounds with all of their initial intensity. The personal slights, the poignant disappointments, the rending heartaches—all the shadows of the past that tend to thwart our spiritual effectiveness and growth—are best forgotten. Thank God if you have a good "forgetter." Such forgetting is something that each of us needs to cultivate.

On the other hand, there are some things that should be remembered. The children of Israel, after 40 years of hardship in the wilderness, stood at last on the verge of entering the Promised Land, which flowed with milk and honey. In the wilderness they had depended on the Lord God for food and water, and health and protection. Now they would enjoy the good things of the land of Canaan. And Moses, the servant of God, knowing human nature, warned them *not* to forget the Lord to whom they owed so much.

Our own Pilgrim fathers did not forget to thank God in the days when our nation was young. But has our familiarity with ease and comfort bred forgetfulness? "Beware," said Moses, "lest thou forget" (Deut. 6:12). And his message to ancient Israel is a message to us today.[16]

—Paul T. Culbertson
1905-93
Educator

Sin Is a Rebellion

John Wesley's classic definition of sin as a "willful transgression of a known law of God" is often quoted but widely misunderstood. At first blush one gets the impression that sin is a legalistic matter, the simple fact of breaking a law. It is because Wesley's critics mistake him to be saying this that they criticize him for not taking sin seriously.

But Wesley was a much better theologian than that. This definition really points to the attitude that underlies any lawbreaking, an attitude of rebelliousness, or as 1 John 3:4 puts it when properly translated, "Sin is lawlessness" (NASB, NIV, RSV, cf. NEB).

From the biblical perspective, this "lawlessness" roots in man's refusal to accept his role as creature (created being) with the consequent attempt to become his own god. In a word it is self-sovereignty.[17]

—William M. Greathouse
1919-
Seminary President and General Superintendent

Practicing Holiness

Sanctification or perfect love is not simply a doctrine to be embraced, nor an experience to be enjoyed in some isolated cloister, but a practical heart condition with which to meet the conditions of life, and that we should not simply be passively good, but actively good, and do "more than others." A hothouse holiness will not last long amid the chilling atmosphere and biting frosts of an opposing world.

Holiness is exceedingly practical. It has to do with every aspect of life. "Be ye holy *in all manner of conversation*" (1 Pet. 1:16, italics added) both in our relationship with God and in our relationships with our fellowman. They who would be right with God must be right with men. It is utterly impossible to be right with God and wrong with our fellowman. "If a man say, I love God, and hateth his brother, he is a liar" (1 John 4:20). This term "brother" does not simply refer to such as may be fellow members of the same organization or church, but to our fellowman in general. Malice and hatred, and the perfect love of God cannot abide in the same heart.

Those who say they forgive the offense but cannot forget, and continue to avoid the offender, stand self-convicted, in that they are doing just as others—sinners—are doing.[18]

—**C. W. Ruth**
1865—1941
Associate Pastor to Bresee

A Holy Life—a Heart Issue

What a man is in his heart of hearts, in the secret citadel of his being, can be measured by what he loves and hates. Jesus loved His Father with a perfect love and loved righteousness as a corollary of His love for the Father. As a further corollary He hated unrighteousness and iniquity with a perfect hatred. So will we if we are conformed to His image.

It is not our profession but our preferences that determine the real quality of our character. What looks good to us? What appeals to us? What is attractive to us? A holy person will find within himself a growing revulsion toward wickedness and evil wherever he sees it, in whatever form he finds it.[19]

—**Richard S. Taylor**
1912-
Theologian and Seminary Professor

The Holy Spirit's Surprises

It was the Holy Spirit to whom our fathers and mothers of the Church of the Nazarene related themselves. He is the Dynamic.

He will not be harnessed. He will not submit to our wills. He is creative and bursts out, like a raging fire, from the strictures we may try to build about Him.

Our heritage does not tie us to the past, but harnesses us to a dynamic that propels us into the demands of the future faster than we are often prepared to go. If we follow Jesus, who is "the same yesterday, and to day, and for ever" (Heb. 13:8), we will have to put on seven-league boots and use them. Jesus is not behind us; He is a long way ahead of us.[20]

—**Mildred Bangs Wynkoop**
1905-97
Theologian

9 ❋ "Be Calm in Thy Soul"
The Inner Dimension of Holiness

Jesus connected the believer's inner and outer life together as shown in this passage recorded by John: "On the final and climactic day of the Feast, Jesus took his stand. He cried out, 'If anyone thirsts, let him come to me and drink. Rivers of living water will brim and spill out of the depths of anyone who believes in me this way, just as the Scripture says.' (He said this in regard to the Spirit, whom those who believed in him were about to receive. The Spirit had not yet been given because Jesus had not yet been glorified.)" (John 7:37-39, TM).

Of course, the human experience of holiness has often been made lopsided, sometimes destructively so, by those who neglected the inner life to be holy activists. Others took an equally extreme though opposite view that inner piety in a withdrawn setting was true holiness, a kind of monastery approach to holy living. Both positions taken to the extreme are puny and cause great problems for the Christian. True holiness starts inside but shows in conduct.

A holy inner life moves us from contemplation and prayer to action. It is reporting for duty, an action shaped by a heart focused on Jesus. Be assured that the inner life clarifies the action God wants us to take. The devotional writer Thomas Kelly puts the message in a wonderfully clear, inspiring two-sentence summary, "There is a center to which we must all return. Eternity is at our hearts, pressing upon our time-torn lives, warning us with intimations of our astounding destiny, calling us home unto Itself."[1]

After you have prayed, go to work and observe in amazement what God will do through you.

—Neil B. Wiseman

Faith Is a Matter of the Heart

Faith is a prerequisite to a happy relationship with God. "But without faith it is impossible to please him; for he that cometh to God must believe that he is, and that he is a rewarder of them that diligently seek him" (Heb. 11:6).

Faith is simply taking God at His word and acting as if we did. Faith is an invisible force unmeasured in strength but simple in operation. The promise of God and obedience to God are basic factors in the operation of faith, and place within reach of the Christian unlimited resources.

The 11th chapter of Hebrews presents a long list of the heroes of faith and their victories: wars were won, walls were broken down, cities were conquered, fires were quenched, lions were tamed, natural laws were suspended, choices were made, and far-reaching plans executed. What testimonials to the triumph of faith!

Faith is the Christian's chief weapon of defense against fear, worry, and satanic assaults. "Above all, taking the shield of faith, wherewith ye shall be able to quench all the fiery darts of the wicked" (Eph. 6:16).

Faith is timeless, always the same, available to every generation. We today may reap the fruit of faith even as others have in the past. Our "Red Seas," "walled cities," "fiery furnaces," and "lions' dens" are different but nevertheless very real. Strong, harassing forces and pressures invade every Christian's "little world"— home, business, social, or public life. His safe refuge is in the promise: "God is faithful, who will not suffer you to be tempted above that ye are able; but will with the temptation also make a way to escape, that ye may be able to bear it" (1 Cor. 10:13).

Faith is a microscope with which one may discern God's fingerprints on current events, reassuring him that God has not forgotten to be faithful.

Faith is a periscope that enables the Christian to see over steep mountains and around sharp corners, revealing glorious victories emerging from what he thought were today's defeats. By faith he draws courage to labor on and patiently wait for the golden harvest.

A place of full assurance amid a world of chaos is found in a life committed to God, with faith in God's plan and in His power to execute it.

"This is the victory that overcometh the world, even our faith" (1 John 5:4).[2]

—D. I. Vanderpool
1891—1988
General Superintendent

Sometimes Love Must Be Tough

Love is "happiness." Happiness is not an emotional titillation, but a harmony of the whole of the self. Holiness is not a glorified maladjustment, a neurosis, as its critics like to say. It is health, vitality, wholeness; the end of disharmony, edginess, and out-of-jointness. Love goes straight to the heart of personal relationships and demands a right ground for fellowship. It mercilessly, but healingly, sorts out the motives and directs the realignment of attitudes and relationships. It stands in judgment against any attitude or act that, in its name and claiming its authority wrongly, destroys fellowship. It is not soft, but highly discriminating. It is not blind, but keenly alert to anything that ruptures fellowship. It is not amorphous, unrelated to law, but the very inner structure of moral law, the conservator of moral integrity.

Love is never superficial. It always deals with key issues. It sorts out the central from peripheral matters in its zeal to create and preserve the true relationship. It stands guard over self-esteem lest it inadvertently slip into selfishness. It protects personal integrity from an overconcern about personal rights.[3]

—Mildred Bangs Wynkoop
1905-97
Theologian

Integrity and Authenticity

Deep-inside goodness reaches into the grass roots of our being. It penetrates the inmost and the utmost, clear to the foundation of our lives. This is related to our being authentic and real persons. In deep-inside goodness there is no compromise with shoddiness, shallowness, or superficiality.

One must go against the currents of modern society to maintain and develop this type of goodness. The prevailing standard of conduct, according to the "11th commandment," is, "Don't get caught." The emphasis is on the smooth operator who covers his clues so well that no one suspects what is lurking inside his heart. It shows up in polishing the apple, twisting the wrist, and buttering up people. We sometimes try to make these ways of manipulating people acceptable by calling them diplomacy, cleverness, and shrewdness. However, if we labeled them correctly, diplomacy would often be duplicity, cleverness would probably be pretense, and shrewdness would sometimes be sham.

When the grace of the Lord invades our whole being, all trace of these artificial tactics is eliminated. This goodness makes us real persons—so transparent that no shadow is cast upon our sincerity. We rate our sense of being authentic persons above social status, job status, and material status. We figure that if we lost everything we owned and retained our integrity, we would come out ahead.[4]

—Mendell Taylor
1912—2000
Seminary Professor

Intentional Growth in Holiness

All normal life is marked by growth. Whenever growth totally stops, death begins. The body and the mind that cease to develop commence to die. And this is true of the spiritual nature. To "grow in grace, and in the knowledge of our Lord and Saviour Jesus Christ" (2 Pet. 3:18) is not a matter of choice but of necessity.

But traveling the way of holiness does not just happen. It isn't the aimless wandering of a tramp. It takes effort and purpose to make a journey and to arrive at a desired destination. We must resist the idea that where we are is where we should stay for the rest of our lives. True, it is easier to drift than to travel. It is comforting to camp among familiar scenes, to linger over victories already won. But the call of God's far horizons is upon us, and we must not stay.[5]

—W. T. Purkiser
1910-92
Editor and College President

Temptation and the Sanctified

The erroneous idea is very persistent that the sanctified teach the impossibility of temptation of those who claim the experience of holiness. This has never been taught by any recognized man. In fact, I do not believe it has ever been taught by anyone within the Holiness movements of the earth. The fact is, the cleaner one is, the purer is his life, the closer he tries to walk with God, the harder and the more desperately will Satan fight him in order to destroy his soul and break down the influence of his life.

As long as we are human, so long will we be tempted. But, thank God, there is a power given from above that makes us more than conquerors. We cannot escape being tempted, but we are not forced to yield.[6]

—R. T. Williams Sr.
1883—1946
General Superintendent

A Holy Way to Think

I often wonder what we have missed in life because we did not think. How much hurt has been done because we did not think before we spoke or acted! Many are the admonitions in the Word to think. This one passage (Phil. 4:8) lists six things to think on. Only one can we emphasize: "Whatsoever things are true." No time should be given to thinking on things that are false. The things that are true demand our sober consideration.

Think on the things that are true about prayer. "In every thing by prayer and supplication with thanksgiving let your requests be made known unto God" (v. 6). Think on the partnership in all things by prayer. For the Lord has entered into everything of our life.

Then let us think on the truth of power. "I can do all things through Christ which strengtheneth me" (v. 13). We must never fail to think on the strength that God assures us we shall find in His grace. We have no cause to plead weakness. All may overcome through the Christ of our strength. Power for the trials, power for the tasks, and power to triumph in all of life. Think on these things. Never let them escape your attention.[7]

—T. M. Anderson
1888–1929
Pastor and Evangelist

———— ⚎ ————

Take My Will and Make It Thine

Take my will. It is easier to say, "Take my hands, take my feet, take my voice." And it is more temporary. We use them only on occasion. There is a finality about saying, "Take my will." This represents a constant state of mind, a maintained attitude of surrender, of yielding, of resignation, of giving up.

Why is it so hard to say, "Take my will"? Why is it so hard to maintain that attitude?

Probably it is because of fear. Fear of the unknown. Fear of just what this surrender involves. We do not understand, sometimes we have not been told, that in giving Him our wills, they are not to be broken, or even bent. They are to be blended with His will—His all-seeing, all-knowing will. Our horizons are so circumscribed. We see only the realities of this little life, and we sometimes have a false concept of God the Father. He is not trying to force us into doing something that is wholly distasteful to us or for which we are by nature unprepared. He has made us. His will is on our side. He knows our potential. He wants to bring us to the point of greatest fulfillment, of supreme joy and happiness, not only for this brief span of years we are to spend on earth but for all eternity.[8]

—Audrey J. Williamson
1899—1994
Educator and Writer

Christ—the Organizing Center

How shall we find life's highest happiness? The psychiatrist answers in two words—"personal integration." If we are to be wholesome personalities, life must be organized around some central goal and purpose. The consecrated life is reasonable in view of the requirements for mental health. Consecration demands of us an all-inclusive commitment—and a commitment to life's supreme value. Sooner or later devotion to anything less than God and goodness will fall short of our deepest needs. The highest unification of life and the only permanently successful integration of personality is in the realm of the Spirit. Jesus gives us the clue: "Seek ye first the kingdom of God" (Matt. 6:33).

The Bible tells us that "a double-minded man is unstable in all his ways" (James 1:8). The psychiatrist adds that this instability destroys our happiness. Certainly to live a divided life, to feel pulled apart and at loose ends, to be all at odds with oneself, is to be unhappy. On the other hand, as Dr. William H. Shelton says, "Happiness is essentially a state of going somewhere, wholeheartedly, one directionally, without regret or reservation." How else in life can one find such happiness? This radiance of living is made possible by entire consecration. Full devotion to the will of God is our reasonable service, for through consecration comes fullness of life.[9]

—A. F. Harper
1907-
Editor

Character Never Goes Out of Date

Character is the only commodity that never fluctuates in value. The price of wheat, corn, cotton, and silk rises or falls according to the law of supply and demand; but not so of character. Its value is always the same. The market is never overstocked, and the demand never diminishes. Material things perish; the waste and wear of time, the forces of disintegration, crumble our earthly building into ruin, but the name and influence of a great and good man never die. The time will come when St. Peter's will not exist; but the time will never come when the world will cease to remember and hold in highest esteem its builder, Michelangelo. Character is as eternal as the throne of God, and its influence knows no limit. The power of good character touches, inspires, and continues forever, and its value is ever the same.

Character is supreme, kingly, divine—the first in time and first in eternity. A noble soul has almost infinite resources and riches within himself—faculties and virtues that are Godlike when drawn out. As the mountain unlocks her golden treasures at the magic touch of man, as the sea yields her pearls to the determined seeker for hidden wealth, the soul of a good man will reveal riches in which God finds delight and honor.[10]

—R. T. Williams Sr.
1883—1946
General Superintendent

Holiness Grows Great Souls

God needs big people to do His work. And everything holiness is, is geared to making big people. Only big people can handle big visions. Only big people, who have known the depth of doubt and have found truth, can handle truth. To handle big truths it is necessary to have a flexible, growing, enlargable self. If we have terminated our expandability and have limited our vision, our love, our understanding, our empathy, and our dedication to personal growth alone, we are living on a lower level than the divine call and will never "serve [this] present age, [our] calling to fulfill" (STTL, 536).

Only big people—or people in the process of stretching out their cramped, pinched little souls—can be Christian revolutionaries. Only big people are able to see past the small, petty, childish irritations close to them, out into the real problems that tear at the heart of the world.

Small people attack each other, tear each other to pieces, and think they are doing God's service. Exhausting our fighting spirit in destroying those among us who differ with us gives a false sense of achievement and fosters a bitter, divisive spirit.[11]

—Mildred Bangs Wynkoop
1905-97
Theologian

Character Matters at Home Too

Character is made up of sincerity, moral integrity, honesty, and solid ideals of life. Character is what a man or woman is inside. It is what a person is when he is alone or in the anonymity of a crowd away from home. The test of character, it has been said, is what you would do if you knew it never would be found out.

Shoddy character may be covered by a facade of pretense for a while, but sooner or later its weaknesses will come to light. No amount of smooth talk or fair speech can hide or make up for a basic lack of goodwill and fundamental honor and integrity.[12]

—W. T. Purkiser
1910-92
Editor and Professor

Radical Love—the Spirit of Our Lord

No amount of noisy radicalism or loud profession of red-hot religion will ever take the place of the gracious Spirit of the Master. The champions of old-fashioned, radical holiness must be exponents of a spirituality that is genuine and deep. When men stoop to the use of bitter, biting, stinging sarcasm and show a spirit of jealousy and hate and are ready to split hairs and hang heretics, it is evident that they are themselves void of the Spirit of Christ.

The Church of Jesus Christ must be radical against sin in all of its forms and should steadfastly resist the encouragement of worldliness, but in doing so we must not fail to manifest the Spirit of Christ who has given us this religion. "If any man have not the Spirit of Christ, he is none of his" (Rom. 8:9).[13]

—H. B. Garvin
d. 1974
Pastor

The Inner Secrets of Spiritual Health

What a fine example Caleb provided. The hour had come when Israel was to receive her inheritance in Canaan. It happened that the division came right during Caleb's 85th birthday.

What a wonderful illustration of spiritual vigor and health! He testified that God had kept him for 45 years since Kadesh-barnea. And on his birthday he was able to say that he was as strong to go out and to come in as he was at 40 years of age. And to climax it all, he requested the land possessed by the giant Anakims.

But there was a secret to it as there always is. In fact, there were two essential reasons why Caleb had kept so well spiritually.

The first reason was that his was a heart religion—in the hour of test he had kept his heart in a right attitude (Josh. 14:7). A right heart attitude is always a basic requirement for spiritual health. This will guarantee the heart against deteriorating influences that weaken and destroy.

The other secret of Caleb's spiritual health is revealed in the verse "I wholly followed the LORD my God" (v. 8)—he wholly followed God. His was an unswerving and final allegiance that had long since been settled. Though there were murmurings all about, and aside from Joshua he had to stand alone, he had settled it to go with God. You and I, too, if we would keep spiritually strong and fully alive, must keep a right heart attitude and wholly follow God. This is the secret of real spiritual health.[14]

—H. V. Miller
1894—1948
General Superintendent

Then All with Me Will Be Well

Let me pray as the days go by;
Let me live with my faith on high;
Let me walk with my Savior nigh—
Then all with me will be well.

Let me read so much of His Word
That my thoughts dwell long on my Lord;
Let me not of my service hoard—
Then all with me will be well.

Then the storm of the ages may blow,
And the world her wild seed may sow,
But onward t'ward heaven I go—
Then all with me will be well.

Chorus:
Then all with me will be well,
No matter what tomorrow may bring;
For my Christ is the Master of all—
To my Rock and my Fortress I'll cling.[15]

—V. H. Lewis
1912—2000
General Superintendent

Bud Robinson's Daily Prayer

O Lord, give me a backbone as big as a sawlog,
And ribs like the sleepers under the church floor.
Put iron shoes on me and galvanized breeches,
And give me a rhinoceros hide for a skin;
And hang a wagon load of determination up in the gable end of my soul.

And help me to sign the contract to fight the devil as long as I have got a fist, and bite him as long as I've got a tooth, and then gum him till I die.

All this I ask, for Christ's sake.
Amen.[16]

—Bud Robinson
1860—1942
Evangelist

My Last Message to the Church

My last message to all my people, ministry, and laity is that they seek until they have found the conscious, abiding, manifesting experience that Jesus insists upon in the verses found in Matt. 5:43-46, inclusive, not in word only "but in deed and in truth" (1 John 3:18); so shall Jesus be glorified.

"You have heard that it was said, 'Love your neighbor and hate your enemy.' But I tell you: Love your enemies and pray for those who persecute you, that you may be sons of your Father in heaven. He causes his sun to rise on the evil and the good, and sends rain on the righteous and the unrighteous. If you love those who love you, what reward will you get? Are not even the tax collectors doing that?" (Matt. 5:43-46, NIV).[17]

—Phineas F. Bresee
1838—1915
Founding General Superintendent

Notes

Preface

1. Source unknown.

Chapter 1

1. Phineas F. Bresee, *Herald of Holiness,* 4 November 1931, front cover.

2. J. B. Chapman, *Herald of Holiness,* 4 November 1931, 7.

3. Lon Woodrum, *The Kingdom Beyond* (Kansas City: Beacon Hill Press, 1949), 60.

4. Lawrence B. Hicks, "The Blessing," *Herald of Holiness,* 27 September 1948, 6.

5. Quoted in *The Nazarene Pulpit: A Collection of Sermons from Well-Known Preachers* (Kansas City: Nazarene Publishing House, 1925), 113.

6. Bud Robinson, *Bud Robinson's Religion, Philosophy, and Fun* (Kansas City: Beacon Hill Press, 1942), 46.

7. H. Orton Wiley, *Herald of Holiness,* 2 September 1931, 2.

8. W. T. Purkiser, *Herald of Holiness,* 16 March 1966, 10.

9. C. W. Ruth, "The Distinctive Note," *Herald of Holiness,* 27 July 1927, 5.

10. Quoted in A. F. Harper, *Holiness and High Country* (Kansas City: Beacon Hill Press, 1964), 206.

11. Orval J. Nease, *A Vessel unto Honor* (Kansas City: Beacon Hill Press, 1952), 45.

12. G. B. Williamson, *Holiness for Every Day* (Kansas City: Beacon Hill Press of Kansas City, 1980), 126-27.

13. Wes Tracey, ed., *The Redeemed Will Walk There: Sermons on the Life of Holiness from the Chapel of Nazarene Theological Seminary* (Kansas City: Beacon Hill Press of Kansas City, 1983), 205.

14. E. F. Walker, *Sanctify Them* (1899; reprint, Kansas City: Beacon Hill Press of Kansas City, 1968), 45-46.

15. *Nazarene Pulpit,* 234-35.

16. C. Warren Jones, *Herald of Holiness,* 14 September 1960, 4.

17. H. E. Jessop, *We—The Holiness People* (Chicago: Chicago Evangelistic Institute, 1948), 93-94.

18. Jack Ford, *What the Holiness People Believe* (Cheshire, England: Emmanuel Bible College and Missions, n.d.), 28.

19. Richard S. Taylor, *A Right Conception of Sin* (Kansas City: Beacon Hill Press, 1945), 109.

20. Phineas F. Bresee, "The Great Question," sermon preached before 1903, printed in a booklet of sermons, Roach, Chandler, and Roach Religious Publications.

21. Charles A. McConnell, "Ye Shall Receive Power," *Herald of Holiness,* 8 June 1942, back cover.

22. C. William Fisher, *Wake Up and Live* (Kansas City: Beacon Hill Press, 1955), 27.

23. C. W. Ruth, "Some Lessons for the Sanctified to Learn," *Herald of Holiness,* 24 August 1935, 5.

24. Quoted in William E. McCumber, ed., *Great Holiness Classics,* vol. 5 (Kansas City: Beacon Hill Press of Kansas City, 1989), 146-47.

25. Harper, *Holiness and High Country,* 87-88.

Chapter 2

1. Samuel Young, *God Makes a Difference* (Kansas City: Beacon Hill Press, 1954), 51-52.

2. W. E. McCumber, *Take a Bible Break* (Kansas City: Beacon Hill Press of Kansas City, 1986), 72.

3. Bertha Munro, *Strength for Today* (Kansas City: Beacon Hill Press, 1954), 56.

4. Quoted in J. Fred Parker, ed., *Lift Up Thine Eyes* (Kansas City: Beacon Hill Press of Kansas City, 1969), 37.

5. N. B. Herrell, *Herald of Holiness,* 10 July 1929, 10.

6. J. G. Morrison, "Stewardship of Prayer," *Herald of Holiness,* 3 April 1929, 10.

7. Bob Benson, *See You at the House* (Nashville: Generoux Press, 1986), 29.

8. E. O. Chalfant, "Intensified Devotions," *Herald of Holiness,* 3 April 1929, 7.

9. Quoted in James R. Spruce, comp., *A Simple Faith: Insights for Living in a Complex World* (Kansas City: Beacon Hill Press of Kansas City, 1997), 90-91.

10. R. V. DeLong, *Mastering Our Midnights* (Kansas City: Beacon Hill Press, 1953), 37-38.

11. Source unknown.

Chapter 3

1. B. V. Seals, *Beside the Shepherd's Tent* (Kansas City: Beacon Hill Press, 1956), 13.

2. D. Shelby Corlett, *Herald of Holiness,* 5 October 1935, front page.

3. Bud Robinson, *Bees in Clover* (Kansas City: Nazarene Publishing House, 1921), 102-3.

4. Parker, *Lift Up Thine Eyes,* 28-29.

5. Richard S. Taylor, *Life in the Spirit* (Kansas City: Beacon Hill Press of Kansas City, 1966), 217.

6. J. B. Chapman, *Let the Winds Blow* (Kansas City: Beacon Hill Press, 1957), 49.

7. Parker, *Lift Up Thine Eyes,* 34-35.

8. Chapman, *Let the Winds Blow,* 54.

9. H. V. Miller, *The Gladness of God* (Kansas City: Beacon Hill Press, 1944), 74-75.

10. Parker, *Lift Up Thine Eyes,* 36-37.

11. W. Shelburne Brown, *Herald of Holiness,* 17 August 1966, 8.

12. Olive M. Winchester, "Wesley on Christian Joy," *Herald of Holiness,* 31 August 1935, 5.

13. H. Orton Wiley, *The Pentecostal Promise* (Kansas City: Beacon Hill Press, 1963), 17.

14. D. I. Vanderpool, *Herald of Holiness,* 6 December 1961, 2.

15. Mendell Taylor, *Every Day with Paul* (Kansas City: Beacon Hill Press of Kansas City, 1978), 198-99.

16. Munro, *Strength for Today,* 249.

17. *Nazarene Pulpit,* 174-75.

18. J. B. Chapman, *Singing in the Shadows* (Kansas City: Nazarene Publishing House, 1941), 94.

19. Fletcher Galloway, *Bible School Journal,* 22 April 1947, 38.

20. Hugh C. Benner, *Herald of Holiness,* 13 February 1963, inside front cover.

21. Source unknown.

22. Parker, *Lift Up Thine Eyes,* 21.

23. Lon R. Woodrum, *Herald of Holiness,* 6 April 1942, back cover.

Chapter 4

1. Quoted in Rebecca Davis and Susan Mesner, eds., *The Treasury of Religious and Spiritual Quotations* (Pleasantville, N.Y.: Reader's Digest Association, 1994), 54.

2. J. B. Chapman, *Christ and the Bible* (Kansas City: Beacon Hill Press, 1940), 19-21.

3. Hardy C. Powers, *Pilot Points of the Church of the Nazarene* (Kansas City: Nazarene Publishing House, 1958), 10-11.

4. *Nazarene Pulpit,* 74-75.

5. Ralph Earle, *How We Got Our Bible* (Kansas City: Beacon Hill Press of Kansas City, 1971), 17.

6. Young, *God Makes a Difference,* 121.

7. C. W. Ruth, *Entire Sanctification Explained* (Kansas City: Beacon Hill Press, 1955), 73.

8. A. M. Hills, *Herald of Holiness,* 10 March 1926, 6.

9. Spruce, *Simple Faith,* 111.

Chapter 5

1. J. B. Chapman, "A Nazarene Manifesto" (prayer offered at the Superintendents' Conference, Kansas City, January 5-6, 1944), 4.

2. R. T. Williams, *The Perfect Man* (Peniel, Tex.: Peniel Book Co., 1913), 125.

3. "General Superintendents' Quadrennial Address to the 10th General Assembly," *Herald of Holiness,* 22 June 1940, 24-25.

4. Ibid., 25.

5. V. H. Lewis, *The Church Winning Souls* (Kansas City: Beacon Hill Press of Kansas City, 1983), 67.

6. Hugh C. Benner, *Rendezvous with Abundance* (Kansas City: Beacon Hill Press, 1958), 46-47.

7. H. Orton Wiley, *Herald of Holiness,* 4 January 1933, back cover.

8. Munro, *Strength for Today,* 46.

9. John E. Riley, *Herald of Holiness,* 9 June 1965, 11.

10. J. B. Chapman, *Herald of Holiness,* 19 August 1925, front cover.

11. Parker, *Lift Up Thine Eyes,* 88.

12. D. I. Vanderpool, *Living Waters* (Kansas City: Nazarene Publishing House, 1964), 16-18.

13. H. Orton Wiley, "Worship God," *Herald of Holiness,* 9 September 1931, 2.

14. J. G. Morrison, *Herald of Holiness,* 20 August 1930, 17.

15. H. Orton Wiley, "The Dignity of the Local Church," *Herald of Holiness,* 7 August 1929, 2.

Chapter 6

1. Mother Teresa, *A Gift for God* (San Francisco: Harper and Row, 1975), 29.

2. Sylvester T. Ludwig, *Come Ye Apart* (1941), May 23 devotional.

3. Young, *God Makes a Difference,* 101.

4. J. B. Chapman, *All Out for Souls* (Kansas City: Beacon Hill Press, 1946), 16-17.

5. McCumber, *Great Holiness Classics,* 123.

6. Phineas F. Bresee, "The Last Command," *Herald of Holiness,* 9 October 1929, front page.

7. Taylor, *Every Day with Paul,* 215.

8. "Quadrennial Address," 25.

9. Mildred Bangs Wynkoop, *A Theology of Love* (Kansas City: Beacon Hill Press of Kansas City, 1972), 29-30.

10. Williamson, *Holiness for Every Day,* 92-93.

11. W. E. McCumber, *The Bible Speaks to Me About My Beliefs* (Kansas City: Beacon Hill Press of Kansas City, 1989), 83.

12. J. B. Chapman, *Herald of Holiness,* 13 January 1926, 2.

13. Harper, *Holiness and High Country,* 193.

14. George Coulter, *Herald of Holiness,* 27 April 1966, inside front cover.

15. Brian L. Farmer, *Herald of Holiness,* 2 February 1966, 3.

16. Lewis, *Church Winning Souls,* 20.

17. J. G. Morrison, "Common Loyalty," *Herald of Holiness,* 30 September 1925, 3-4.

18. W. T. Purkiser, *Come Ye Apart* (1954), May 15 devotional.

19. Mildred Bangs Wynkoop, *John Wesley: Christian Revolutionary* (Kansas City: Beacon Hill Press of Kansas City, 1970), 32.

Chapter 7

1. Paul S. Rees, *The Face of Our Lord* (Grand Rapids: Wm. B. Eerdmans Publishing Company, 1951), 110-11.

2. Paul J. Stewart, *Come Ye Apart* (1953), April 24 devotional.

3. Quoted in Harold Ivan Smith, ed., *The Quotable Bresee* (Kansas City: Beacon Hill Press of Kansas City, 1983), 33.

4. J. B. Chapman, "What Is It to Be Spiritual?" *Herald of Holiness,* 22 February 1928, front cover.

5. H. Orton Wiley, *God Has the Answer* (Kansas City: Beacon Hill Press, 1956), 27.

6. Fred M. Weatherford, "The Supreme Life," *Herald of Holiness,* 27 April 1942, 6.

7. Woodrum, *Kingdom Beyond,* 69.

8. Source unknown.

9. Kathryn Blackburn Peck, *Herald of Holiness,* 27 April 1942, 7.

10. J. G. Morrison, "Stewardship of Prayer," *Herald of Holiness,* 3 April 1929, 11.

11. A. M. Hills, *Herald of Holiness,* 11 September 1929, 6.

12. Parker, *Life Up Thine Eyes,* 12.

13. Milo L. Arnold, "Unadulterated Marriage," *Herald of Holiness,* 16 October 1968, 3.

14. T. M. Anderson, *Herald of Holiness,* 13 November 1929, 8.

15. Munro, *Strength for Today,* 43.

16. Taylor, *Life in the Spirit,* 100.

17. Howard W. Jerrett, "The Blight of Ordinariness," *Herald of Holiness,* 20 October 1926, 11.

18. McCumber, *Great Holiness Classics,* 154-55.

Chapter 8

1. Mother Teresa, *Life in the Spirit* (Cambridge: Harper and Row of San Francisco, 1983), 9.

2. A. S. London, "One of the Seven Deadly Sins," *Herald of Holiness,* 22 June 1927, 5.

3. Bertha Mae Lillenas, *Come Ye Apart* (1942), July 30 devotional.

4. D. Shelby Corlett, "Mountain Peaks of the Bible," *Herald of Holiness*, 3 April 1929, 17.

5. W. Shelburne Brown, *Come Ye Apart* (1953), January 10 devotional.

6. Milo Arnold, *Life Is So Great, I Really Don't Want to Get Off* (Grand Rapids: Zondervan Publishing House, 1975), 13.

7. Harry E. Jessop, *Come Ye Apart* (1951), January 21 devotional.

8. H. H. Wise, *Come Ye Apart* (1947), December 30-31 devotional.

9. Lewis T. Corlett, *Come Ye Apart* (1947), January 29-30 devotional.

10. Haldor Lillenas, *Come Ye Apart* (1947), May 17 devotional.

11. *Nazarene Pulpit*, 218-19.

12. Wynkoop, *John Wesley: Christian Revolutionary*, 52.

13. William E. McCumber, *Holiness Preachers and Preaching*, vol. 5 (Kansas City: Beacon Hill Press of Kansas City, 1989), 78.

14. Ross Price, *Come Ye Apart* (1943), August 23 devotional.

15. A. L. Parrott, *Come Ye Apart* (1943), May 22 devotional.

16. Paul T. Culbertson, *Come Ye Apart* (1943), June 30 devotional.

17. William M. Greathouse and H. Ray Dunning, *An Introduction to Wesleyan Theology* (Kansas City: Beacon Hill Press of Kansas City, 1989), 57.

18. C. W. Ruth, *Herald of Holiness*, 22 June 1940, 17-18.

19. Taylor, *Life in the Spirit*, 73.

20. Wynkoop, *John Wesley: Christian Revolutionary*, 11.

Chapter 9

1. Bob and Michael Benson, *Disciplines for the Inner Life* (Waco, Tex.: Word, 1985), 13.

2. D. I. Vanderpool, "The Triumph of Faith," *Herald of Holiness*, 2 August 1961.

3. Wynkoop, *Theology of Love*, 28.

4. Taylor, *Every Day with Paul*, 264.

5. Harper, *Holiness and High Country*, 233.

6. R. T. Williams, *A Neglected Theme (Temptation)* (Kansas City: Nazarene Publishing House, 1930), 77.

7. Parker, *Lift Up Thine Eyes*, 30.

8. Audrey J. Williamson, *Take My Life* (Kansas City: Beacon Hill Press of Kansas City, 1982), 43-44.

9. Harper, *Holiness and High Country*, 126.

10. Williams, *The Perfect Man*, 12-13.

11. Wynkoop, *John Wesley: Christian Revolutionary*, 44-45.

12. W. T. Purkiser, "Foundations of the Home," *Herald of Holiness*, 5 September 1962, inside front cover.

13. H. B. Garvin, "Paragraph Sermons," *Herald of Holiness,* 1 July 1929, 6.
14. H. V. Miller, *Come Ye Apart* (1941), October 11 devotional.
15. Source unknown.
16. Source unknown.
17. Smith, *Quotable Bresee,* 223.